The
ESSENTIAL
LEWIS AND
CLARK

WILLIAM CLARK

MERIWETHER LEWIS

The
ESSENTIAL
LEWIS AND
CLARK

LANDON Y. JONES, *Editor*

ecco

An Imprint of HarperCollinsPublishers

Portraits of Meriwether Lewis and William Clark by Charles Wilson Peale, courtesy of Independence National Historical Park.

HarperCollins books may be purchased for educational, business, or sales promotional use. For information please e-mail the Special Markets Department at SPsales@harpercollins.com.

First Ecco paperback edition published 2002

Designed by Elliott Beard

Library of Congress Cataloging-in-Publication Data has been applied for.

ISBN 0-06-019600-9

ISBN 0-06-001159-9 (pbk.)

17 ❖/RRD 20

For my father, Landon Y. Jones Sr., who led my first
exploration of the West

With special thanks to the officers and members of the
Lewis and Clark Trail Heritage Society Inc.,
P.O. Box 3434, Great Falls, MT 59403

CONTENTS

Contents

A Note on the Text

The journals of Lewis and Clark were written by the captains during their expedition on a daily basis and expanded when time allowed. But while Clark recorded an entry about virtually every day of the expedition, Lewis fell dismayingly silent for long stretches of time. No one knows why. "Perhaps he was depressed," Stephen Ambrose wonders, "or maybe it was just a severe case of writer's block." Or perhaps he did write faithfully, without interruption, and these journals were lost and will turn up someday in an attic.

After delays resulting from Lewis's personal problems and eventual death in 1809, the journals and field notes were first prepared for publication by Nicholas Biddle, a young Philadelphia lawyer. In 1810, Biddle personally interviewed William Clark and other members of the party, and consulted written accounts of the expedition to fill out his narrative. (Sergeant Patrick Gass had published his journal in 1807.) Biddle's largely paraphrased work was published in 1814 in a two-volume edition of fewer than two thousand copies. Clark did not receive his own copy for two years. Meanwhile, a busy industry of dime novels and mawkish retellings had already sprung up around the two captains' adventures. Full versions of the journals have since been edited by Elliott Coues (1893), Reuben Gold Thwaites (1904–05) and Gary Moulton (1983–2000).

The excerpts in this volume are drawn entirely from Thwaites's *Original Journals of the Lewis and Clark Expedition*. Parsing the excerpts in this volume from an original of more than 900,000 words is like filling a teacup with a fire hose; much has spilled over. However, there was much duplication in the original, since the captains freely copied over each other's entries for safekeeping. They also kept copious celestial and navigational data, as well as recording abundant scientific information requested by Jefferson. This edition has dropped all of that material in order to focus on the human drama of the voyage, as told by the two captains. (Sergeants Floyd, Gass and Ordway also kept less complete journals, as did Private Whitehouse.) Readers interested in the complete journals of Lewis and Clark are urged to consult Gary Moulton's excellent twelve-volume edition published by the University of Nebraska Press.

For reasons of consistency and convenience, the volume numbers and chapter headings here follow the nomenclature used by Thwaites and Biddle. This editor has not hesitated to delete entire sections, paragraphs, and sentences within a single day's entry. Ellipses have been frequently added for clarity, but longer deletions have not been indicated. Handwritten notes made on the pages of the original manuscripts by Biddle and other editors are indicated by parentheses and italics. Many of Thwaites's original footnotes have been retained and are indicated with "Ed." Others have been added by the present editor; they are marked "LYJ." Other footnotes are cited to the particular source.

The picturesque capitalization, punctuation, and spelling of the captains is a challenge for every editor. This edition retains the original spellings, in all their rococo glory, but has regularized the capitalizations and corrected the punctuation.

INTRODUCTION

As Meriwether Lewis and William Clark approached the Pacific Ocean in November 1805 their rejoicing was unbounded. "Ocian in view! O! the joy," exulted Clark, who strained to hear the breaking of the waves on the distant shore he had sought for so long.

How do we know this?

We know it because Clark pulled out an elkskin-bound field journal he carried at his side every day and wrote it down. We also know that Clark had sore feet, that Lewis suffered from bouts of melancholia, that their fingers were cold, and that they had to eat dogs and colts to survive. We know that the dangers faced by their party of thirty-three included hunger, disease, subzero temperatures, blizzards, boiling rapids, furious grizzly bears, and unending plagues of mosquitoes. We know that they met dozens of diverse tribes of Native Americans, described countless plants and animals new to science, and recorded acts of astounding courage and compassion. They wrote all these remarkable things down in the journals they kept stored in tin boxes in wooden boats and canoes that all too frequently were drenched in river water.

In keeping their meticulous journals, Lewis and Clark were faithfully following the instructions of their commander-in-chief, Thomas Jefferson. Jefferson had long fancied an exploration of the lands beyond the Mississippi. As early as 1783 he had proposed the journey to George Rogers Clark, William's older brother. But it was not until he became president and successfully negotiated the Louisiana Purchase in April 1803 that his voyage of discovery became a reality. Earlier that year Congress had already authorized $2,500 for an expedition whose purpose, Jefferson said, was simple: to find "the direct water communication from sea to sea formed by the bed of the Missouri and perhaps the Oregon."

To ensure the mission's success, Jefferson put in charge a trusted family friend from Virginia, Meriwether Lewis. An army captain well versed in frontier life, Lewis prepared for the exploration literally at the side of Jefferson, living in the White House while detached from the army and serving as the president's private secretary. At Jefferson's urging, he traveled to Philadelphia to study science, medicine, and navigation with the leading scholars of the time. He then recruited as his cocaptain a man he admired greatly, William Clark, who had commanded the army company Lewis had served in as an ensign during the Indian campaigns. In 1803, Clark was thirty-three, and Lewis was just twenty-nine. Though Lewis was technically the commanding officer, and Clark never received his promised captain's commission, both leaders concealed that fact from the men. Throughout their journey Lewis and Clark treated one another as equals.

The written record the captains kept would be critical to the success of their journey. In order to justify an expedition originally meant to go through Spanish territory, Jefferson had claimed it would be "a literary pursuit" designed to add knowledge about natural history and geology. His real agenda was to capture the flourishing Canadian fur trade from the British and to establish America's territorial claims to the Oregon coast. Jefferson's expansionist ambitions had already been galvanized by another book: the publication in 1801 of Alexander Mackenzie's *Voyages from Montreal*, the Scottish explorer's account of his audacious journey across Canada to the Pacific coast in 1793. Mackenzie's book established a British claim to the Northwest coast, and Lewis and Clark would later carry a copy of Mackenzie's book on their own journey.

When the captains returned to St. Louis in September 1806 after twenty-eight months and eight thousand miles, they were greeted with awe and rejoicing by the citizens—even though, literally speaking, they had not succeeded in fulfilling Jefferson's objectives. What was once thought to be an easy water route across the continent had actually proved to be an unthinkable portage of 220 miles across the most formidable mountains in North America. Historians today question whether their journey made a difference in opening the Oregon territory to America's westward expansion. They certainly were not the first Europeans in the West; there were Spanish brands on the Shoshone horses Lewis and Clark saw. But if Jefferson was disappointed that his principal objective for the expedition proved chimerical, he quickly consoled himself by contemplating the astonishing amount of information Lewis and Clark had brought back about the vast territory up the Missouri.

That information is known to us today from a single source: the nearly one million published words of the Lewis and Clark journals. Every day of their journey, working under nearly unbearable conditions, the two captains kept careful notes about the astonishing things they had seen and done. They mapped every turn of the rivers they traveled, using both dead reckoning and celestial observations. They wrote detailed descriptions of flora and fauna. They carefully described the ethnography of the many tribes of Native Americans they encountered.

Jefferson, the quintessential man of the Enlightenment, had asked them to do all that, and they did it well. They were in essence the first journalists to travel the West, writing down their own first rough draft of history. As Gary Moulton has pointed out, their journey is set apart from all other frontier legends by the credibility and narrative sweep of the evidence— the journals themselves.

But adventuring and record-keeping alone do not account for the mesmerizing power of their words. During their journey, and in their journals, Lewis and Clark created an epic, one whose effect on our collective imagination has made it, over time, the unofficial *Odyssey* of American history. Like the Greek hero, Lewis and Clark embarked on a voyage into the unknown that took them away from home and family so long that they were given up for dead. Theirs is not merely a diary of a journey; it is a heroic saga complete with powerful characters, enraged monsters, violent conflicts, startling twists in plot, wry humor, and unexpected acts of compassion. As any heroic epic should, their own journey prefigured in microcosm the westward expansion of an entire people.

In this journey there was not one bard but two. With the bipolar perspective comes depth and range. Each writer extends the other; each observer throws the other into sharper relief; each act is seen through another's eyes. Clark is magnified by Lewis's words; Lewis is enhanced by Clark's.

On one level, Lewis is the more sophisticated storyteller, composing long, erudite entries on everything from botany to blue beads. If the Voyage of Discovery had been told only by Lewis it would have been rich in science, natural history, and rhetoric. Clark, on the other hand, is blunter, earthier, and more to the point; his story crackles with emotion, action, and drama. Lewis's sensibility is poetic and discursive; Clark's is cinematic. The contrast between their two voices— and their more than occasional role reversals—fills what otherwise would be one-dimensional narratives with tension and energy.

The structure of the journals is symphonic. Upriver from St.

Louis the themes introduce themselves quietly, as the explorers push languidly through a pastoral setting. There are occasional floating trees and collapsing riverbanks, but most days float by quietly. The journal entries are short, framed by word repetitions; the recurring phrase, "We proceeded on," returns to the narrative as reliably as a Homeric epithet, reassuring us that even this perilous a voyage can have a predictable routine to it.

The most arresting events of the journey are presaged by foreboding leitmotifs. The explorers hear tales of the grizzly bears and see their frighteningly huge tracks before actually encountering one. They see distant smoke and moccasin prints of Indians at Three Forks before actually finding the Shoshones days later. They mistakenly think they see the Pacific Ocean long before they actually taste it.

Meanwhile, the personalities who become the central players of the drama wander in from the wings, one at a time, lingering backstage until their appointed hour. We barely glimpse York, Clark's slave and the only black man on the journey, until he is encountered by the amazed Indians. The Indian girl Sacagawea joins the party at the Mandan Villages and quietly sets about gathering roots. We first meet Cameahwait, the Shoshone chief who will provide the horses the explorers desperately need to cross the Rockies, six days before we discover, in one of American history's most amazing coincidences, that he is Sacagawea's brother.

The prose style mirrors the action. As the explorers approach the journey's moment of truth—the dramatic meeting with the Shoshones at the Continental Divide—time suddenly slows. Lewis's journal entries become longer and longer as his rising excitement energizes his pen. Where he previously wrote dispassionately and objectively, now his entries are crammed with vivid details and moment-to-moment chronologies. Later, the fight with the Blackfeet is as closely observed and finely detailed as in any screenplay:

I reached to seize my gun but found her gone. I then drew a pistol from my holster and terning myself about saw the Indian making off with my gun. I ran at him with my pistol and bid him lay down my gun which he was in the act of doing when the Fieldses returned and drew up their guns to shoot him which I forbid as he did not appear to be about to make any resistance or commit any offensive act. He droped the gun and walked slowly off. I picked her up instantly.

When Lewis relaxes, his language becomes vigorously idiomatic. He awakes one morning "as hungry as a wolf." He hears women pounding roots and says that the sound "reminds me of a nail factory" (which he had observed years earlier at Monticello). After a filling meal, he remarks, "we once more live in clover." After successfully negotiating with an Indian, Lewis remarks, "I soon found that I had touched him on the right string."

As a stylist and observer of nature, Lewis modeled his writing after his mentor Thomas Jefferson, and specifically after Jefferson's own *Notes on the State of Virginia*, published in 1785. Here, for example, is Jefferson rhapsodizing over Virginia's Natural Bridge: "It is impossible for the emotions arising from the sublime, to be felt beyond what they are here: so beautiful an arch, so elevated, so light, and spring as if it were up to heaven, the rapture of the spectator is really indescribable!"

And here is Lewis's similarly ornate description of the Great Falls of the Missouri: "I wished for the pencil of Salvator Rosa or the pen of Thompson¹ that I might be enabled to give to the enlightened world some just idea of this truly magnificent and sublimely grand object, which has from the commencement of time been concealed from the view of civilized man; but this was fruitless and vain."

Clark, on the other hand, felt no such self-consciousness about his literary aspirations—or the lack of them. His journal entries are peppered with a delightful array of misspellings and grammatical errors, many of them rendered imaginatively and fearlessly. In Clark's pen the single word "Sioux" could become "Scioux," "Seauex," "Seeaux," "Soux," "Suouez," or, best of all, "Cocoux." (Robert Betts has counted twenty-seven different spelling of "Sioux.") On the journey, Clark wore "mockersons," ate "water millions," and slapped away all too many "muskeetors." (In fairness to Clark, even the best educated Americans of the day displayed erratic spelling until Webster's first dictionary proscribed standardized spellings a half-century later.)

It is in Clark's homespun words, however, that the journals convey much of their emotional force. Clark's anger at the Teton Sioux is understated. "I felt myself warm & spoke in verry positive terms," he writes laconically, in a style right out of Owen Wister's *The Virginian*. More often, his words describe acts of compassion. He wraps a sick Indian woman in flannel, divides his meat with hungry Indian families, and upbraids Touissant Charbonneau after he has struck Sacagawea. Writing about Sergeant Charles Floyd, the only man to die during the expedition, Clark is simple and eloquent: "This man at all times gave us proofs of his firmness and determined resolution to doe service to his country and honor to himself."

One of the most persistent images of the Western wilderness—that it is a place with an enhanced moral dimension where individuals acted with both courage and compassion—was born in the journals of Lewis and Clark. Other explorers like Zebulon Pike, John Wesley Powell, and Alexander Mackenzie left behind vivid accounts of the remarkable things they saw and accomplished, but their trips took place in a moral void; they were reporting on the encounter of a single individual with a vast, overwhelming wilderness. Lewis and Clark's journals record for us not only a story of astonishing personal courage but also a powerful parable of trust within a human community. One man nearly falls from a precipice and screams, "God! God! Captain, what shall I do?" His faith in his captain is repaid as Lewis calmly rescues him. The whole party disagrees with the captains at the Marias River, and yet when told to proceed on, "They said very cheerfully that they were ready to follow us any where we thought proper to direct." This is a story of trust—trust shared by the two leaders, trust acknowledged without reservation by the thirty others they led, and trust freely given to them by the individual Indian tribes whose magnanimity did more than anything to guarantee the survival of the explorers.

Today the lasting images of Lewis and Clark are Western archetypes— the solitary moccasin print in the sand, the grizzly bear chasing a buckskinned frontiersman up a tree, an Indian woman helping the Europeans travel through her land, a herd of buffalo hurtling over a cliff, the canoe disappearing around a turn in the river. In a time when America is finding its common purpose elusive, it is not surprising that the sense of mission that drove Lewis and Clark evokes nostalgia and admiration.

Ernest Hemingway once observed that "All modern American literature comes from one book by Mark Twain called *Huckleberry Finn.*" It takes nothing away from Twain's wonderful novel to say that Lewis and Clark were there first. Long before Huck lit out for the territory, Lewis and Clark left just down the river from Twain's home in Hannibal, Missouri, in a trip that actually *defined* the territory. They filled their journals with an authentic vernacular before Twain revolutionized American literature by having Huck tell his story the way people really talked. Like Odysseus, they came home, back from the dead, to a world amazed by their return. What extraordinary things they had seen! That we are able to relive their journey today is thanks to the care they took to write it down.

---

1. Rosa was a seventeeth-century Italian painter; Thomson was an eighteenth-century Scottish poet. —LYJ

THE CORPS OF DISCOVERY

Commanding
Meriwether Lewis, Captain 1ˢᵗ U.S. Infantry
William Clark, Second Lieutenant, U.S. Corps of Artillerists

Sergeants
John Ordway
Nathaniel Pryor
Charles Floyd (died August 20, 1804)
Patrick Gass (appointed August 26, 1804, to replace Floyd)

Interpreters
George Drouillard ("Drewyer")
Toussaint Charbonneau ("Shabowner," "Chabonah," "Charbono")

Privates
William Bratton
John Collins

John Colter
Pierre Cruzatte
Joseph Field
Reuben Field
Robert Frazier
George Gibson
Silas Goodrich
Hugh Hall
Thomas P. Howard
François Labiche
Baptiste Lapage
Hugh NcNeal
John Newman (dropped from party, October 13, 1804)
John Potts
Moses B. Reed (deserted August 4, 1804)
George Shannon
John Shields
John B. Thompson
William Werner
Joseph Whitehouse
Alexander Willard
Richard Windsor
Peter Wiser

Others
York, a slave
Sacagawea, the Shoshone wife of Charbonneau
Jean-Baptiste Charbonneau ("Pomp"), the son of Sacagawea

Also
Seaman ("Scannon"), Lewis's Newfoundland dog

VOLUME ONE

FROM RIVER DUBOIS TO
TWO-THOUSAND-MILE CREEK

May 13, 1804–May 5, 1805

*M*eriwether Lewis and a dozen men left Pittsburgh on August 31, 1803, in a fifty-five-foot masted keelboat and floated down the Ohio River. They stopped at Clarksville, Indiana Territory, to pick up William Clark and more men. After spending the winter of 1803–04 camped at River Dubois, across the Mississippi from St. Louis and the mouth of the Missouri, the captains prepared in the spring to depart for the unexplored lands up the Missouri River. On May 14, Clark left Camp Dubois with perhaps forty-two men in the keelboat and two pirogues (dugout canoes) and proceeded up the river to St. Charles to rendezvous with Lewis, who had been making departure arrangements in St. Louis. The Voyage of Discovery was under way.

[Clark] May 14, 1804

I determined to go as far as St. Charles, a French village 7 leags. up the Missourie, and wait at that place untill Capt. Lewis could finish the business in which he was obliged to attend to at St. Louis and join me by land from that place . . . I set out at 4 oClock P.M, in the presence of many of the neighbouring inhabitants, and proceeded on under a jentle brease up the Missourie.

[Lewis] May 20, 1804

At 10 Ock. a.m. agreably to an appointment of the preceeding day, I was joined by Capt. Stoddard, Lieuts. Milford & Worrell together with Messrs. A. Chouteau, C. Gratiot, and many other rispectable inhabitants of St. Louis, who had engaged to accompany me to the Vilage of St. Charles. Accordingly, after bidding an affectionate adieu to my hostis, that excellent woman the spouse of Mr. Peter Chouteau, and some of my fair friends of St. Louis, we set forward to that vilage in order to join my friend companion and fellow labourer Capt. William Clark, who had previously arrived at that place with the party destined for the discovery of the interior of the continent of North America.

[Clark] May 21, 1804

All the forepart of the day arranging our party and procureing the different articles necessary for them at this place. Dined with Mr. Ducett and set out at half passed three oClock under three cheers from the gentlemen on the bank and proceeded on. . . .

We camped in a bend at the Mo. of a small creek. Soon after we came too the Indians arrived with 4 deer as a present, for which we gave them two qt. of whiskey.

[Clark] May 23, 1804

We passed a large cave called by the French the *Tavern*—about 120 feet wide 40 feet deep & 20 feet high. Many different immages are painted on the rock. At this place the Ind. & French pay omage. Many names are wrote on the rock. Stoped about one mile above for Capt. Lewis who had assended the clifts which is at the said cave 300 fee[t] high, hanging over the waters. . . . Capt. Lewis near falling from the pinecles of rocks 300 feet. He caught at 20 foot. Saved himself by the assistance of his knife.[1]

[Clark] May 24, 1804

Passed a verry bad part of the river called the deavels race ground. This is where the current sets against some projecting rocks for half a mile on the labd. side. . . . The swiftness of current wheeled the boat, broke our *toe* rope, and was nearly over setting the boat. All hands jumped out on the upper side and bore on that side untill the sand washed from under the boat and wheeled on the next bank. By the time she wheeled a 3rd time got a rope fast to her stern and by the means of swimmers was carted to shore.

[Clark] June 16, 1804

The mosquitoes and ticks are noumerous & bad.

[Orderly Book; Clark] Camp
Mouth of the Kansies
June 29, 1804

Ordered—A court martiall will set this day at 11 oClock, to consist of five members, for the trial of *John Collins* and *Hugh Hall*, confined on charges exhibited against them by Sergeant Floyd, agreeable to the articles of war.

DETAIL FOR THE COURT
Sergt. Nat. Pryor presd.
2 John Colter
3 John Newmon
4 Pat. Gass
1 J. B. Thompson

John Potts to act as judge advocate.

The court convened agreeable to order and proceeded to the trial of the prisoners viz John Collins charged "with getting drunk on his post this morning out of whiskey put under his charge as a sentinal, and for suffering *Hugh Hall* to draw whiskey out of the said barrel intended for the party."

To this charge the prisoner plead *not guilty.*

The court after mature deliberation on the evidence adduced &c. are of oppinion that the prisoner is guilty of the charge exibited against him, and do therefore sentence him to receive *one hundred lashes on his bear back.*

Hugh Hall was brought before the court charged with takeing whiskey out of a keg this morning which whiskey was stored on the bank (and under the charge of the guard) contrary to all order, rule, or regulation.

To this charge the prisoner "pleaded guilty."

The court find the prisoner guilty and sentence him to receive *fifty* Lashes on his bear back.

[Clark] June 30, 1804

A verry large wolf came to the bank and looked at us this morning.

[Orderly Book; Lewis]
Camp New Island
July 12, 1804

A court martial consisting of the two commanding officers will convene this day at 1 oCk. p.m. for the trial of such prisoners as may be brought before them; one of the court will act as judge advocate.

[Clark]

The commanding officers, Capt. M. Lewis & W. Clark constituted themselves a court martial for the trial of such prisoners as are guilty of capatal crimes, and under the rules and articles of war punishable by DEATH.

Alexander Willard was brought foward charged with "*lying down and sleeping on his post*" *whilst a sentinal, on the night of* the 11th instant (by John Ordway, Sergeant of the guard)

To this charge the prisoner pleads *guilty of lying down, and not guilty, of going to sleep.*

The court after duly considering the evidence aduced, are of oppinion that the *prisoner* Alex. Willard is guilty of every part of the charge exhibited against him. It being a breach of the *rules* and articles of *war* (as well as tending to the probable destruction of the party) *do sentience* him to receive *one hundred lashes, on his bear back, at four diferent times in equal proportion* and order that the punishment commence this evening at sunset, and continue to be inflicted (by the guard) every evening untill completed.

[Clark] July 30, 1804

From the bluff on the 2nd rise imediately above our camp, the most butifull prospect of the river up & down and the countrey ops. presented itself which I ever beheld; the river meandering the open and butifiall plains, interspursed with groves of timber, and each point covered with tall timber, such as willow cotton sum mulberry, elm, sucamore lynn & ash. The groves contain hickory, walnut, coffee nut & oake in addition.

Joseph Fields killed and brought in an anamale called by the French *brarow*,[2] and by the Ponies *Cho car tooch.* This anamale burrows in the ground and feeds on flesh, (prarie dogs) bugs & vigatables. His shape & size is like that of a beaver, his head mouth &c. is like a dogs with short ears, his tail and hair like that of a ground *hog*, and longer and lighter. His interals like the interals of a hog. His skin, thick and loose, his *Belly* is white and the hair short, a white streek from his nose to his sholders. The hind feet small and toe crooked, his legs are short and when he moves just sufficent to raise his body above the ground. He is of the bear species. We have his skin stuffed.

[Clark] July 31, 1805

The evening verry cool. The musquitors are yet troublesome.

The Indian tribes of the Missouri had been out hunting buffalo on the plains as Lewis and Clark ascended the river. But they finally encountered a small party of Otos and a few Missouris near the present-day Council Bluffs, Nebraska.

[Clark] August 2, 1805

At sunset Mr. Fairfong [Ottoe interpreter resident with them] and a [party] of Otteau & Missourie Nation came to camp. Among those Indians 6 were chiefs. Capt. Lewis & myself met those Indians & informed them we were glad to see them, and would speak to them tomorrow. Sent them some rosted meat, pork flour & meal. In return they sent us water millions. Every man on his guard & ready for any thing.

[Clark] August 3, 1804

Mad up a small preasent for those people in perpotion to their Consiquence, also a package with a meadle to accompany a speech for the grand chief. After brackfast we collected those Indians under an owning of our main sail. In presence of our party paraded & delivered a long speech to them expressive of our journey the wishes of our government, some advice to them and directions how they were to conduct themselves. The principal chief for the Nation being absent, we sent him the speech flag meadel & some cloathes. After hering what they had to say delivered a medal of second grade to one for the Ottos & one for the Missourie and present 4 medals of a third grade to the inferior chiefs two for each tribe. (Those two parts of nations Ottos & Missouries now residing together is about 250 men, the Ottoes composeing 2/3d and Missouris 113 part.)

[Clark] August 12, 1804

A *prarie wolf* come near the bank and barked at us this evening. We made an attempt but could not git him. The animale barkes like a large ferce dog.[3]

The expedition stopped at a village occupied by a tribe of Omahas, recently devastated by a smallpox epidemic.

[Clark] August 14, 1804

The ravages of the small pox (which swept off [about 4 years ago] 400 men & Womin & children in perpopotion) has reduced this nation not exceeding 300 men and left them to the insults of their weaker neighbours, which before was glad to be on friendly turms with them. I am told when this fatal malady was among them they carried their franzey to verry extroadinary length, not only of burning their village, but they put their wives & children to death with a view of their all going together to some better countrey. They burry their dead on the top of high hills and rais mounds on the top of them. The cause or way those people took the small pox is uncertain, the most probable, from some other nation by means of a war party.

[Clark] August 15, 1804

I went with ten men to a creek damed by the beavers about half way to the village. With some small willows & bark we made a drag and hauled up the creek, and cought 318 fish of different kind i.e. pike, bass, salmon, perch, red horse, small cat, and a kind of perch called silver fish on the Ohio. I cought a shrimp prosisely

of shape size & flavour of those about N. Orleans & the lower part
of the Mississippi.

*In mid-August a private, Moses B. Reed, disappeared and was pre-
sumed to have deserted. The captains sent George Drouillard and four
others to bring back "the deserter Reid with order if he did not give up
peaceibly to put him to death." The expedition was near the present-
day Sioux City, Iowa, when Drouillard returned with the captured
Reed and a delegation of Oto chiefs.*

[Clark] August 18, 1804

In the after part of the day the party with the Indians arrivd.
We meet them under a shade near the boat and after a short talk
we gave them provisions to eat & proceeded to the trial of Reed. He
confessed that he "deserted & stold a public rifle, shot-pouch, powder & ball" and requested we would be as favourable with him as
we could consistently with our oathes—which we were and only
sentenced him to run the gantlet four times through the party &
that each man with 9 swichies should punish him and for him not
to be considered in future as one of the party.

The three principal chiefs petitioned for pardin for this man.
After we explained the injurey such men could doe them by false
representations, & explang. the customs of our countrey they were
all satisfied with the propriety of the sentence & was witness to the
punishment.

Cap L. birth day. The evening was closed with an extra gill of
whiskey and a dance untill 11 oClock.

[Clark] August 19, 1804

Serjeant Floyd is taken verry bad all at once with a biliose chor-
lick. We attempt to relieve him without success as yet he gets worst
and we are much allarmed at his situation. All give attention to
him.

[Clark] August 20, 1804

Serjeant Floyd as bad as he can be. No pulse & nothing will stay a moment on his stomach or bowels. Passed two islands on the S. S. [South Side] and at the first bluff on the S. S. Serj. Floyd died with a great deal of composure. Before his death he said to me, "I am going away. I want you to write me a letter." We buried him on the top of the bluff ½ mile below a small river to which we gave his name. He was buried with the Honors of War much lamented. A seeder post with the (1) Name Sergt. C. Floyd died here 20th of August 1804 was fixed at his grave. This man at all times gave us proofs of his firmness and determined resolution to doe service to his countery and honor to himself.[4]

[Clark] August 23, 1804

J. Fields sent out to hunt came to the boat and informed that he had killed a buffalow in the plain a head.[5] Cap. Lewis took 12 men and had the buffalow brought to the boat . . . 2 elk swam the river, and was fired at from the boat. . . . Several prarie wolves seen to day. Saw elk standing on the sand bar. The wind blew hard [west] and raised the sands off the bar in such clouds that we could scercely [see] this sand being fine and verry light stuck to everry thing it touched, and in the plain for a half a mile the distance I was out, every spire of grass was covered with the sand or durt.

[Clark] August 24, 1804

In a northerley detection . . . an emence plain a high hill is situated, and appears of a conic form, and by the different nations of Indians in quarter is suppose to be the residence of Deavels. That they are in human form with remarkable large heads, and about 18 inches high, that they are very watchfull and are arm'd with sharp arrows with which they can kill at a great distance; they are said to kill all persons who are so hardy as to attempt to approach the hill; they state that tradition informs them that many Indians have suffered by those little people, and among others three Mahar men fell a sacrefise to their murceless fury not many years sence. So much do the Maha, Soues, Ottoes and other neighbouring nations believe this fable, that no consideration is suffecient to induce them to approach the hill.

[Clark] August 25, 1804

Capt. Lewis and myself concluded to go and see the Mound which was viewed with such turror by all the different nations in this quarter. . . . The reagular form of this hill would in some measure justify a belief that it owed its orrigin to the hand of man; but as the earth and loos pebbles and other substances of which it was composed, bore an exact resemblance to the steep ground which border on the creek in its neighbourhood we concluded it was most probably the production of nature.

The surrounding plains is open, void of timber and leavel to a great extent, hence the wind from whatever quarter it may blow, drives with unusial force over the naked plains and against this hill; the insects of various kinds are thus involuntaryly driven to the Mound by the force of the wind, or fly to its leeward side for shelter; the small birds whoes food they are consequently resort in great numbers to this place in surch of them; perticularly the small brown martin of which we saw a vast number hovering on the leward side of the hill, when we approached it in the act of catching those insects. They were so gentle that they did not quit the place untill we had arrivd. within a fiew feet of them.

One evidence which the Inds. give for believeing this place to be the residence of some unusial sperits is that they frequently discover a large assemblage of birds about this mound [this] is in my opinion a suffecient proof to produce in the savage mind a confident belief of all the properties which they ascrib [to] it.

From the top of this Mound we beheld a most butifull landscape. Numerous herds of buffalow were seen feeding in various directions; the plain to north N.W. & N.E. extends without interuption as far as can be seen.

As they approached the site of the present Yankton, S.D., the explorers had entered the territory controlled by the large tribe of Yankton Sioux.

[Clark] August 29, 1804

Sergt. Pryor & Mr. Dorion[6] with 5 cheifs and about 70 men & boys arrived on the opposit side. We sent over a perogue & Mr. Dorrion & his son who was tradeing with the Indians came over with Serjt. Pryor, and informed us that the chiefs were there. We sent Serjt. Pryor & young Mr. Dorion with som tobacco, corn and a few kittles for them to cook in, with directions to inform the chiefs that we would speek to them tomorrow . . . a fat dog was presented as a mark of their great respect for the party of which they partook hartily and thought it good and well flavored.

[Clark] August 30, 1804

After prepareing some presents for the cheifs which we intended [to] make by giving meadels, and finishing a speech which we intended to give them, we sent M. Dorion in a perogue for the cheifs and warriers to a council under an oak tree near where we had a flag flying on a high flagstaff.

At 12 oClock we met and Cap. L. delivered the speach & then made one great chiff by giving him a meadel & some cloathes, one 2nd chief & three third chiefs in the same way, they recd. those things with the goods and tobacco with pleasure. To the grand chief we gave a flag and the parole (certificate) & wampom with a hat & chief's coat.

We smoked out of the pipe of peace, & the chiefs retired to a bourey [*bowray*] made of bushes by their young men to divide their presents and smoke eate and council. . . . The Souex is a stout bold looking people (the young men handsom) & well made, the greater part of them make use of bows & arrows. Some fiew fusees I observe among them notwithstanding they live by the bow and arrow. They do not shoot so well as the Nothern Indians. The warriers are verry much deckerated with paint porcupine quills and feathers, large leagins and mockersons, all with buffalow roabs of different colours. The squars wore peticoats & a white buffalow roabe with the black hare turned back over their necks and sholders.

I will here remark a SOCIETY which I had never before this day heard was in any nation of Indians, four of which is at this time present and all who remain of this band. Those who become members of this society must be brave active young men who take a vow never to give back let the danger be what it may. In war parties they always go forward without screening themselves behind trees or anything else. To this vow they strictly adhier dureing their lives.

An instance which happened not long sence, on a party in crossing the Missourie on the ice, a whole was in the ice imediately in their course which might easily have been avoided by going around. The foremost man went on and was lost. The others wer draged around by the party. In a battle with the Crow [Kite] Indians who inhabit the *Cout Noir* or black mountain out of 22 of this society 18 was killed. The remaining four was draged off by their party.

[Clark] September 7, 1804

We landed after proceeding 5½ miles, near the foot of a round mounting, which I saw yesterday, resembling a dome. Capt. Lewis & myself walked up to the top which forms a cone and is about 70 feet higher than the high lands around it. In decending this cupola, discovered a village of small animals that burrow in the grown (those animals are called by the French *Petite Chien*). Killed one and caught one a live by poreing a great quantity of water in his hole.[7] We attempted to dig to the beds of one of those animals. After diging 6 feet, I found by running a pole down that we were not half way to his lodge. We found 2 frogs in the hole, and killed a dark rattle snake near with a ground rat (or prairie dog) in him (those rats are numerous).

The village of those animals covd. about 4 acres of ground on a gradual decent of a hill and contains great numbers of holes on the top of which those little animals set erect make a whistleing noise and whin allarmed step into their hole. We por'd into one of the holes 5 barrels of water without filling it. Those animals are about the size of a small squirel shorter (or longer) & thicker, the head much resembling a squirel in every respect, except the ears which is shorter, his tail like a ground squirel which they shake & whistle when allarmd the toe nails long, they have fine fur & the longer hairs is gray. It is said that a kind of lizard also a snake reside with those animals.

[Clark] September 9, 1804

I walked on shore all this evening with a view to kill a goat[8] or some prarie dogs in the evening after the boat landed. I derected my servent York with me to kill a buffalow near the boat from a numbr. then scattered in the plains. I saw at one view near the river at least 500 buffalow, those animals have been in view all day feeding in the plains. Every copse of timber appear to have elk or deer.

[Clark] September 11, 1804

A cloudy morning . . . I saw a village of barking squirel[9] 970 yds. long and 500 yds. wide situated on a jentle slope of a hill. Those anamals are noumerous. I killed 4 with a view to have their skins stufed.

Here the man who left us with the horses 22 (*16*) days ago
George Shannon; he started 26 Augt.) and has been a head ever since
joined us nearly starved to death.[10] He had been 12 days without
any thing to eate but grapes & one rabit, which he killed by shooting a piece of hard stick in place of a ball. This man supposeing the
boat to be a head pushed on as long as he could. When he became
weak and feable deturmined to lay by and waite for a tradeing
boat, which is expected, keeping one horse for the last resorse.
Thus a man had like to have starved to death in a land of plenty
for the want of bull'itts or something to kill his meat.

[Clark] September 14, 1804

Walked on shore with a view to find an old vulcanoe, said to be
in this neighbourhood by Mr. J. McKey of St. Charles. I walked on
shore the whole day without seeing any appearance of the vulcanoe. In my walk I killed a buck goat of this country [antelope —
Ed.], about the hight of the grown deer, its body shorter the horns
which is not very hard and forks 2/3 up one prong short the other
round & sharp arched, and is imediately above its eyes. The colour
is a light gray with black behind its ears down its neck, and its face
white round its neck, its sides and its rump round its tail which is
short & white: verry actively made, has only a pair of hoofs to each
foot. His brains on the back of his head, his norstrals large, his eyes
like a sheep he is more like the antilope or gazella of Africa than
any other species of goat.

Shields killed a *hare* like the mountain hare of Europe, waigh-
ing 6¼ pounds (altho pore) his head narrow, its ears large.[11]

[Lewis] September 17, 1804

Having for many days past confined myself to the boat, I
determined to devote this day to amuse myself on shore with my
gun. . . . Accordingly before sunrise I set out with six of my best

hunters, two of whom I dispatched to the lower side of Corvus Creek, two with orders to hunt the bottums and woodland on the river, while I retained two others to acompany me in the intermediate country. One quarter of a mile in rear of our camp which was situated in a fine open grove of cotton wood I passed a grove of plumb trees loaded with fruit and now ripe. Observed but little difference betwen this fruit and that of a similar kind common to the Atlantic States. The trees are smaller and more thickly set. This forrest of plumb trees garnish a plain about 20 feet more elivated than that on which we were encamped. This plain extends back about a mile to the foot of the hills one mile distant and to which it is gradually ascending this plane extends with the same bredth from the creek below to the distance of near three miles above parrallel with the river, and it is intirely occupyed by the burrows of the *barking squiril* hertefore described. This anamal appears here in infinite numbers and the shortness and virdu[r]e of grass gave the plain the appearance throughout it's whole extent of beatifull bowling-green in fine order. A great number of wolves of the small kind, halks [hawks —Ed.] and some pole-cats were to be seen. I presume that those anamals feed on this squirrel. . . .

This senery already rich pleasing and beatiful was still farther hightened by immence herds of buffaloe, deer, elk and antelopes which we saw in every direction feeding on the hills and plains. I do not think I exagerate when I estimate the number of buffaloe which could be compre[hend]ed at one view to amount to 3000.

My object was if possible to kill a female antelope, having already procured a male. I pursued my rout on this plain to the west flanked by my two hunters untill eight in the morning when I made the signal for them to come to me which they did shortly after. We rested our selves about half an hour, and regailed ourselves on half a bisquit each and some jirks of elk which we had taken the precaution to put in our pouches in the morning before we set out, and drank of the water of a small pool which had collected on this plain from the rains which had fallen some days before. We had now after various windings in pursuit of several herds of antelopes which we had seen on our way made the distance of about eight miles from our camp.

We found the antelope extremely shye and watchfull insomuch that we had been unable to get a shot at them; when at rest they generally seelect the most elivated point in the neighbourhood, and as they are watchfull and extreemly quick of sight and their sense of smelling very accurate it is almost impossible to approach them within gunshot; in short, they will frequently discover and flee form you at the distance of three miles.

I had this day an opportunity of witnessing the agility and the superior fleetness of this anamal which was to me really astonishing. I had pursued and twice surprised a small herd of seven, in the first instance they did not discover me distinctly and therefore did not run at full speed, tho' they took care before they rested to gain an elivated point where it was impossible to approach them under cover, except in one direction and that happened to be in the direction from which the wind blew towards them; bad as the chance to approach them was, I made the best of my way toward them, frequently peeping over the ridge with which I took care to conceal myself from their view. The male, of which there was but one, frequently incircled the summit of the hill on which the females stood in a group, as if to look out for the approach of danger. I got within about 200 paces of them when they smelt me and fled; I gained the top of the eminence of which they stood, as soon as possible from whence I had an extensive view of the country. The antilopes which had disappeared in a steep reveene now appeared at the distance of a bout three miles . . . so soon had these antelolpes gained the distance at which they had again appeared to my view I doubted at ferst that they were the same that I had just surprised, but my doubts soon vanished when I beheld the rapidity of their flights along the ridge before me. It appeared reather the rappid flight of birds than the mostion of quadrupeds. I think I can safely venture the asscertion that the speed of this anamal is equal if not superior to that of the finest bloodest courser.[12]

Near the site of the present Pierre, S.D., the party camped and prepared for a crucial meeting with the Teton Sioux, the aggressive tribe that controlled all trade and traffic wishing to proceed further up the Missouri.

[Clark] September 25, 1804

Raised a flag staff & made a orning or shade on a sand bar in the mouth of Teton River, for the purpose of speeking with the Indians. . . . Met in council at 12 oClock and after smokeing, agreeable to the useal custom, Cap. Lewis proceeded to deliver a speech which we were obliged to curtail for want of a good interpeter. All our party paraded. . . . Envited those cheifs on board to show them our boat and such curiossities as was strange to them. We gave them ¼ a glass of whiskey which they appeared to be verry fond of, sucked the bottle after it was out & soon began to be troublesom. One the 2d. cheif assumeing drunkness, as a cloake for his rascally intentions. I went with those cheifs (*in one of the perogues with 5 men—3 & 2 Ind*) (which left the boat with great reluctiance) to shore with a view of reconsileing those men to us.

As soon as I landed the perogue three of their young men seased the cable of the perogue, (*in which we had pressents &c.*) the chiefs soldr. [each Chief has a soldier] huged the mast, and the 2nd chief was verry insolent both in words & justures (pretended drunkenness & staggered up against me) declareing I should not go on, stateing he had not receved presents sufficent from us. His justures were of such a personal nature I felt myself compeled to draw my sword (and made a signal to the boat to prepare for action).

At this motion Capt. Lewis ordered all under arms in the boat. Those with me also showed a disposition to defend themselves and me. The grand chief then took hold of the roap & ordered the young warrers away. I felt myself warm & spoke in verry positive terms. Most of the warriers appeared to have ther bows strung and took out their arrows from the quiver. As I (being surrounded) was not permited (by them) to return, I sent all the men except 2 inps [interpreters] to the boat. The perogue soon returned with about 12 of our determined men ready for any event this movement caused a no. of the Indians to withdraw at a distance, (leaving their chiefs & soldiers alone with me).

Their treatment to me was verry rough & I think justified roughness on my part. They all lift my perogue, and councild. with themselves. The result I could not lern and nearly all went off. After remaining in this situation some time I offered my hand to the 1. & 2. chiefs who refusd. to receve it. I turned off & went with my men on board the perogue. I had not prosd. more the [than] 10 paces before the 1st cheif 3rd & 2 brave men waded in after me. I took them in & went on board. We proceeded on about 1 mile & anchored out off a willow island.

Placed a guard on shore to protect the cooks & a guard in the boat, fastened the perogues to the boat. I call this island Bad Humered Island as we were in a bad humer.

The next morning the party headed four miles up the river before putting to shore at the village of Black Buffalo, chief of the Brule band of the Teton Sioux.

[Clark] September 26, 1804

Set out early proceeded on and came to by the wish of the chiefs for to let their squars [squaws] & boys see the boat and suffer them to treat us well. Great numbers of men womin & children on the banks viewing us. These people shew great anxiety. They appear spritely, generally ill looking & not well made their legs [& arms] small generally, [*high cheek bones, prominent eyes*] they grese &-black [*paint*] themselves [*with coal*] when they dress [*the distingd. men*] make use of a hawks feathers [*Calumet feather adorned with porcupine quills & fastened to the top of the head & falls backwards*] about their heads. the men [*wear*] a robe & each a polecats skin, for to hold ther *Bawe roley* [*Bois roule*] for smoking,[13] fond of dress & show badly armed with fusees, &c.

The squaws are chearfull fine look'g womin not handsom. High cheeks dressed in skins a peticoat and roab which foldes back over ther sholder, with long wool. Do all their laborious work & I may say perfect slaves to the men, as all squars of nations much at war, or where the womin are more noumerous than the men.

After comeing too Capt. Lewis & 5 men went on shore with the cheifs, who appeared disposed to make up & be friendly. After Captain Lewis had been on shore about 3 hours I became uneasy for fear of deception & sent a serjeant to see him and know his treatment which he reported was friendly, & they were prepareing for a dance this evening . The[y] made frequent selicitiations for us to remain one night only and let them show their good disposition towards us. We deturmined to remain. After the return of Capt. Lewis, I went on shore. On landing I was receved on a elegent painted B.[uffalo] robe & taken to the village by 6 men &, was not permited to touch the ground untill I was put down in the grand concill house on a white dressed robe. I saw several Maha prissners and spoke to the Chiefs [telling them that] it was necessary to give those prisoners up & become good friends with the Mahas if they wished to follow the advice of their great father.

I was in several lodges neetly formed as before mentioned as to the Baureily (*Bois brule*—Yankton) tribe. I was met (*on landing from the boat*) by about 10 well dressd young men who took me up in a roabe highly adecrated and set me down by the side of their chief on a dressed robe in a large council house. This house formed a ¾ circle of skins well dressed and sown together under this shelter about 70 men set forming a circle. In front of the cheifs a plac of 6 feet diameter was clear and the pipe of peace raised on (forked) sticks (about 6 or 8 inches from the ground) under which there was swans down scattered. On each side of this circle two pipes, the (two) flags of Spain 2 & the flag we gave them in front of the grand chief.

A large fire was near in which provisions were cooking, in the center about 400lb of excellent buffalo beef as a present for us. Soon after they set me down, the men went for Capt Lewis brought him in the same way and placed him also by the chief. In a fiew minits an old man rose & spoke aproveing what we had done &informing us of their situation requesting us to take pity on them &c. which was answered. The great chief then rose with great state [speaking] to the same purpote as far as we could learn & then with great solemnity took up the pipe of peace & after pointing it to the heavins, the 4 quarters of the globe & the earth, he made some disertation, (*then made a speech*) lit it and presented the stem to us to smoke.

When the principal chief spoke with the pipe of peace he took in one hand some of the most delicate parts of the dog which was prepared for the fiest & made a sacrefise to the flag. After a smoke had taken place, & a short harange to his people, we were requested to take the meal (*& then put before us the dog which they had been cooking, & Pemitigon* [pemmican] *& ground potatoe in several platters. Pemn. is Buffa. meat dried or jerked pounded & mixed with grease raw. Dog Sioux think great dish used on festivals. Eat little of dog—pemn & pote. good.*) We smoked for an hour (till) dark & all was cleared away a large fire made in the center, about 10 musitions playing on tambereens (*made of hoops & skin stretched*), long sticks with deer & goats hoofs tied so as to make a gingling noise, and many others of a similer kind.

Those men began to sing, & beet on the tamboren. The women came finward highly deckerated in their way, with the scalps and tropies of war of their fathers husbands brothers or near connections & proceeded to dance the War Dance (women only dance jump up & down—five or six young men selected accompanied with songs the tamborin making the song extempore words & music every now & then one of the comy. come out & repeat some exploit in a sort of song. This taken up by the young men and the women dance to it) which they done with great chearfullness untill about 12 oClock when we informed the cheifs that they were [*must be*] fatigued [*amusing us*] &c. They then retired & we accompd by 4 cheifs returned to our boat. They stayed with us all night. Those people have some brave men which they make use of as soldiers. Those men attend to the police of the Village. Correct all errors. I saw one of them to day whip 2 squars, who appeared to have fallen out. When he approachd all about appeared to flee with great turrow [terror]. At night they keep two 3, 4 ,5 men at different distances walking around damp singing the accurrunces of the night.

In this tribe I saw 25 squars and boys taken 13 days ago in a battle with the Mahars. In this battle they destroyd 40 lodges, killed 75 men, & som boys & children, & took 48 prisoners womin & boys which they promis both Capt. Lewis and my self shall be delivered up to Mr. Durion at the Bous rulie (*Bois brulé*) tribe. Those are a retched and dejected looking people. The squars appear low & corse but this is an unfavourable time to judge of them.

[Clark] September 27, 1804

I rose early after a bad nights sleep. Found the cheifs all up, and the bank as useal lined with spectators. We gave the 2 great cheifs a blanket a peace, or rether they took off agreeable to their custom the one they lay on and each one peck of corn . . . after staying about half an hour, I went with them on shore. Those men left the boat with reluctience. I went first to the 2 cheifs lodge, where a croud came around. After speeking on various subjects I went to a principal mans lodge from them to the grand Chiefs lodge, after a fiew minits he invited me to a lodge within the circle in which I stayed with all their principal men untill the dance began, which was similer to the one of last night performed by their women with poles (*in their hands*) on which scalps of their enemies were hung, some with the guns, spears & war empliments of (*taken by*) their husbands [*&c.*] in their hands.

Capt. Lewis came on shore and we continued untill we were sleepy & returned to our boat. The 2nd chief & one principal man accompanied us. Those two Indians accompanied me on board in the small perogue. Capt. Lewis with a guard still on shore. The man who steered not being much acustomed to steer, passed the bow of the boat & the peroge came broad side against the cable & broke it which obliged me to order in a loud voice all hands up & at their ores. My preemptry order to the men afid the bustle of their getting to their ores allarmd the cheifs, together with the appearance of the men on shore. As the boat turnd the cheif hollowaed & allarmed the camp or town informing them that the Mahars was about attacking us (*them*). In about 10 minits the bank was lined with men armed the 1st cheif at their head. About 200 men appeared and after about ½ hour returned all but about 60 men who continued on the bank all night, the cheifs contd. all night with us.

This allarm I as well as Capt. Lewis Considered as the signal of their intentions (which was to stop our proceeding on our journey and if possible rob us). We were on our guard all night. The misfortune of the loss of our anchor obliged us to lay under a falling bank much exposd to the accomplishment of their hostile intentions. P. C. [Pierre Cruzatte] our Bowman who cd. speek Mahar informed us in the night that the Maha prisoners informed him we were to be stoped. We shew as little signs of a knowledge of their intentions as possible all prepared on board for any thing which might hapen. We kept a strong guard all night in the boat. No sleep.

[Clark] September 28, 1804

We deturmined to proceed on. With great difficulty got the chiefs out of out boat, and when we was about settingb out the class called the soldiers took possession of the cable. The 1ˢᵗ chief which was still on board, & intended to go a short distance up with us. I told him the men of his nation set on the cable. He went out & told Capt. Lewis who was at the bow. The men who set on the roap was soldiers, and wanted tobacco. Capt. L. would not agree to be forced into any thing. The 2ⁿᵈ chief demanded a flag & tobacco which we refusd to give, stateing proper reasons to them for it.

After much dificuelty—which had nearly reduced us to necessity to hostilities—I threw a carrot of tobacco to 1ˢᵗ chief. Took the port fire from the gunner.[14] Spoke so as to touch his pride. The chief gave the tobacco to his soldiers & her jurked the rope from them and handed it to the bowsman. We then set out under a breeze. About 2 miles up we observed the 3ʳᵈ chief on shore beckining to us. We took him on board. He informed us the roap was held by the order of the 2ⁿᵈ chief who was a double spoken man.

The party continued on to a long island in the Missouri, home to three villages of the Arikara tribe. The captains soon arranged a council with them.

[Clark] October 10, 1804

At 1 oClock the cheifs all assembled & after some little cerremony the council commenced. We informd them what we had told the other before, i.e. Ottoes & Seaux. Made 3 chiefs, 1 for each village. Gave them presents. After the council was over we shot the air guns which astonished them much. They then departed and we rested secure all night.

Those Indians wer much astonished at my servent. They never saw a black man before. All flocked around him & examined him from top to toe. He carried on the joke and made himself more turribal than we wished him to doe.[15]

[Clark] October 12, 1804

A curious custom with the Souix as well as the rickeres is to give handsom squars to those whome they wish to show some acknowledgements to. The Seauex we got clare of without taking their squars; they followed us with squars two days. The Rickores we put off dureing the time we were at the towns but 2 [handsom young] squars were sent by a man to follow us. They came up this evening, and pursisted in their civilities.[16]

[Lewis] October 13, 1804

The court martial convened this day for the trial of John Newman, charged with having uttered repeated expressions of a highly criminal and mutinous nature; the same having a tendency not only to distroy every principle of military discipline, but also to alienate the affections of the individuals composing this detatchnient to their officers, and disaffect them to the service for which they have been so sacredly and solemnly engaged. The prisonar plead not guilty to the charge exhibited against him. The court after having duly considered the evidence aduced, as well as the defence of the said prisonor, are unanimously of opinion that the prisonor John Newman is guilty of every part of the charge exhibited against him, and do sentence him agreeably to the rules and articles of war, to receive seventy five lashes on his bear back, and to be henceforth discarded from the permanent party engaged for North Western discovery . . .

[Clark] October 14, 1804

At 1 oClock we halted on a sand bar & after dinner executed the sentence of the court martial so far as giveing the corporal punish-

ment, & proceeded on a few miles. . . . The punishment of this day
allarmd the Indian chief verry much, he cried aloud (or effected to
cry). I explained the cause of the punishment and the necessity (of
it) which he(also) thought examples were also necessary, & he himself had made them by death. His nation never whiped even their
children, from their burth.

[Clark] October 15, 1804

At sunset we arrived at a camp of Recares of 10 lodges . . . Capt.
Lewis and my self went with the chief who accompanis us, to the
huts of several of the men all of whome smoked & gave us something
to eate . . . also some meat to take away. Those people were kind and
appeared to be much plsd at the attentioned paid them. Those people
are much pleased with my black servent. Their womin verry fond of
carressing our men &c.

[Clark] October 20, 1804

Our hunters killed 10 deer & a goat to day and wounded a
white bear. I saw several fresh tracks of those animals which is 3
times as large as a man's track.[17]

*Farther up the Missouri, north of present-day Bismarck, the Voyage
of Discovery came upon what would become their winter home: the
complex of five villages of Mandans and Hidatsas that was the center of
Indian trade for the Northern Plains.*

[Clark] October 24, 1804

We saw one of the Grand Chiefs of the Mandins, with five lodges
hunting. This chief [Big White] met the chief of the *Ricares* who
accompanied us. With great cordiallity & serimony smoked the pipe
& Capt. Lewis with the interpeter went with the chiefs to his lodges
at 1 mile distant.

[Clark] October 25, 1804

Several Indians came to see us this evening, amongst others the sun of the late great chief of the Mandins (mourning for his father), this man has his two little fingers off; on inquireing the cause, was told it was customary for this nation to show their greaf by some testimony of pain, and that it was not uncommon for them to take off 2 smaller fingers of the hand.

[Clark] November 2, 1805

This morning at daylight I went down the river with 4 men to look for a proper place to winter proceeded down the river three miles & found a place well supld with wood.

[Clark] November 4, 1804

We continud to cut down trees and raise our houses.[18] A Mr. Chaubonie (Chaboneau), interpeter for the Gross Ventre nation, came to see us, and informed that he came down with several Indians from a hunting expedition up the river, to here [hear] what we had told the Indians in council. This man wished to hire as an interpiter.[19]

[Clark] November 6, 1804

Last night late we wer awoke by the sergeant of the guard to see a Nothern light, which was light, (but) not red, and appeared to darken and some times nearly obscured, and open . . . many times appeared in light streeks, and at other times a great space light & containing floating collomns which appeared to approach each other & retreat leaveing the lighter space.

[Clark] November 9, 1804

A verry hard frost this morning. We continue to build our cabens, under many disadvantages. . . . The Mandans graze their horses in the day on grass, and at night give them a stick (an arm-full) of cotton wood (boughs) to eate. Horses dogs & people all pass the night in the same lodge or round house, covd with earth with a fire in the middle. Great number of wild gees pass to the south, flew verry high.

[Clark] November 22, 1804

I was allarmed about 10 oClock by the sentinal, who informed that an Indian was about to kill his wife in the interpeters fire about 60 yards below the works. I went down and spoke to the fel-low about the rash act which he was like to commit and forbid any act of the kind near the fort. Some misunderstanding took place between this man & his fife [wife] about 8 days ago, and she came to this place, & continued with the squars of the interpeters, (he might lawfully have killed her for running away) 2 days ago. She returned to the vill'ge. In the evening of the same day she came to the interpeters fire appearently much beat, & stabed in 3 places. We detected that no man of this party have any intercourse with this woman under the penalty of punishment.

He the husband observed that one of our serjeants slept with his wife & if he wanted her he would give her to him. We derected the serjeant (Odway) to give the man some articles, at which time I told the Indian that I believed not one man of the party had touched his wife except the one he had given the use of her for a nite, in his own bed. No man of the party should touch his squar, or the wife of any Indian, nor did I believe they touch a woman if they knew her to be the wife of another man, and advised him to take his squar home and live hapily together in future.

[Clark] December 7, 1804

The Big White, grand chief of the 1st village, came and informed us that a large drove of buffalow was near and his people was wating for us to join them in a chase. Capt. Lewis took 15 men & went out joined the Indians, who were at the time he got up killing the buffalow on horseback with arrows which they done with great dexterity. His party killed 10 buffalow, five of which we got to the fort by the assistance of a horse in addition to what the men packed on their backs.

[Clark] December 8, 1804

The thermometer stood at 12 degrees below 0, which is 42° below the freesing point. . . . Several men returned a little frost bit, one of [the] men with his feet badly frost bit. My servents feet also frosted &- his P-s [penis] a little.

[Clark] December 21, 1804

The Indian whome I stoped from commiting murder on his wife, thro jellosy of one of our interpeters, came & brought his two wives and shewed great anxiety to make up with the man with whome his joulussey sprung. A womon brought a child with an abcess on the lower part of the back, and offered as much corn as she could carry for some medison. Capt. Lewis administered &c.

[Clark] December 25, 1804

I was awakened before day by a discharge of 3 platoons from the party and the French. The men merrily disposed, I give them all a little taffia and permited 3 cannon fired, at raising our flag. Some men went out to hunt & the others to danceing and continued untill 9 oClock p.m. when the frolick ended &c.

[Clark] January 3, 1804

Several Indians visit us to day & a Gross Ventre came after his wife, who had been much abused, & came here for protection.

[Clark] January 5, 1805

A buffalow dance (or medeson) (*medecine*) for 3 nights passed in the 1ˢᵗ village. . . . The old men arrange themselves in a circle & after smoke[ing] a pipe which is handed them by a young man dress[ed] up for the purpose. The young men who have their wives back of the circle go [each] to one of the old men with a whining tone and request the old man to take his wife (who presents [herself] necked except a robe) and (or sleep with her). The girl then takes the Old Man (who verry often can scarcely walk) and leades him to a convenient place for the business, after which they return to the lodge.

If the old man (or a white man) returns to the lodge without gratifying the man & his wife, he offers her again and again. It is often the case that after the 2ⁿᵈ time without kissing the husband throws a new robe over the old man &c. and begs him not to dispise him & his wife. (We sent a man to this medisan dance last night, they gave him 4 girls.) All this is to cause the buffalow to come near so that they may kill them.

[Clark] January 10, 1805

The Indians of the lower villege turned out to hunt for a man & a boy who had not returnd from the hunt of yesterday, and borrow'd a slay to bring them in expecting to find them frosed to death. About 10 oClock the boy about 13 years of age came to the fort with his feet frosed and had layed out last night without fire with only a buffalow robe to cover him. The dress which he wore was a pr. of cabra (antelope) legins, which is verry thin and mockersons. We had his feet put in cold water and they are comeing too.

Soon after the arrival of the boy, a man came in who had also stayed out without fire, and verry thinly clothed. This man was not the least injured. customs & the habits of those people has anured [them] to bare more cold than I thought it possible for man to endure.

[Clark] January 20, 1805

A missunderstanding took place between the two inturpeters on account of their squars. One of the squars of Shabowner being sick, I ordered my servent to give her some root stewed and tee at dift. times which was the cause of the missundst.

[Clark] January 26, 1805

One man taken violently ad with the plurisie. Bleed & apply those remedies common to that disorder.

[Clark] January 27, 1805

I bleed the man with the plurisy to day & swet him. Capt. Lewis took off the toes of one foot of the boy who got frost bit some time ago.

[Lewis] February 3, 1805

The situation of our boat and perogues is now allarming. They are firmly inclosed in the ice and almost covered with snow. The ice which incloses them lyes in several stratas of unequal thicknesses which are separated by streams of water. This [is] peculiarly unfortunate because so soon as we cut through the first strata of ice the water rushes up and rises as high as the upper surface of the ice and thus creates such a debth of water as renders it impracticable to cut away the lower strata which appears firmly attatched to, and confining the bottom of the vessels. The instruments we have hitherto used has been the ax only, with which, we have made several attempts that proved unsuccessfull from the cause above mentioned.

We then determined to attempt freeing them from the ice by means of boiling water which we purposed heating in the vessels by means of hot stones, but this expedient proved also fruitless, as every species of stone which we could procure in the neighbourhood partook so much of the calcareous genus that they burst into small particles on being exposed to the heat of the fire.

We now determined as the dernier resort to prepare a parsel of iron spikes and attatch them to the end of small poles of convenient length and endeavour by means of them to free the vessels from the ice. We have already prepared a large rope of elkskin and a windless by means of which we have no doubt of being able to draw the boat on the bank provided we can free [it] from the ice.[20]

[Lewis] February 11, 1805

About five Oclock this evening one of the wives of Charbono was delivered of a fine boy.[21] It is worthy of remark that this was the first child which this woman had boarn, and as is common in such cases, her labour was tedious and the pain violent. Mr. Jessome informed me that he had freequently administered a small portion of the rattle of the rattlesnake, which he assured me had never failed to produce the desired effect, that of hastening the birth of the child. Having the rattle of a snake by me I gave it to him and he administered two rings of it to the woman broken in small pieces with the fingers and added to a small quantity of water. Whether this medicine was truly the cause or not I shall not undertake to determine, but I was informed that she had not taken it more than ten minutes before she brought forth. Perhaps this remedy may be worthy of future experiments, but I must confess that I want faith as to it's efficacy.

[Clark] February 13, 1805

I returned last night from a hunting party much fatigued, haveing walked 30 miles on the ice and through points of wood land in which the snow was nearly knee deep . . . walking on uneaven ice has blistered the bottoms of my feat, and walking is painfull to me.

[Clark] February 23, 1805

The father of the boy whose feet were frosed near this place, and nearly cured by us, took him home in a slay.

[Clark] March 17, 1805

Mr. Chabonah sent a Frenchman of our party [to say] that he was sorry for the foolish part he had acted and that if we pleased he would accompany us asgreeabley to the terms we had perposed and doe every thing we wished him to doe &c. &c. He had requested me some thro our French inturpeter two days ago to excuse his simplicity and take him into the cirvice. After he had taken his things across the river we called him in and spoke to him on the subject. He agreed to our tirms and we agreed that he might go on with us &c. &c.

At the end of the winter at Fort Mandan, the captains prepared for the next stage of their journey. To date, they had traveled in lands already mapped by others before them. But now the Missouri would take them into land unknown to white Americans. They had questioned the Mandans and Hidatsas extensively about what to expect. Before leaving, they packed the keelboat and sent it back to St. Louis filled with letters, copies of their journals, scientific and geographical reports, Indian artifacts and vocabularies, and hundreds of mineral, botanical, and animal specimens, including a living prairie dog and magpie. Lewis told Thomas Jefferson that the Indians had assured them that they could cross the Continental Divide a portage of "half a day." And he assured his mother, Lucy Marks, back in Virginia, that during his journey in the months ahead "I feel myself perfectly as safe as I should do in Albemarle; and the only difference between 3 or 4 thousand miles and 130, is that I can not have the pleasure of seeing you as often as I did while at Washington."

[Lewis] April 7, 1805

Having on this day at 4 p.m. completed every arrangement necessary for our departure, we dismissed the barge and crew with orders to return without loss of time to St. Louis.

Our vessels consisted of six small canoes, and two large perogues. This little fleet, altho' not quite so respectable as those of

Columbus or Capt. Cook, were still viewed by us with as much pleasure as those deservedly famed adventurers ever beheld theirs; and I dare say with quite as much anxiety for their safety and preservation. We were now about to penetrate a country at least two thousand miles in width, on which the foot of civilized man had never trodden. The good or evil it had in store for us was for experiment yet to determine, and these little vessells contained every article by which we were to expect to subsist or defend ourselves. However, as the state of mind in which we are, generally gives the colouring to events, when the immagination is suffered to wander into futurity, the picture which now presented itself to me was a most pleasing one.

Entertaining as I do, the most confident hope of succeeding in a voyage which had formed a darling project of mine for the last ten years, I could but esteem this moment of my departure as among the most happy of my life. The party are in excellent health and sperits, zealously attached to the enterprise, and anxious to proceed; not a whisper of murmur or discontent to be heard among them, but all act in unison, and with the most perfect harmony.

I took an early supper this evening and went to bed. Capt. Clark myself the two interpretters and the woman and child sleep in a tent of dressed skins. This tent is in the Indian stile, formed of a number of dressed buffaloe skins sewed together with sinues. It is cut in such manner that when foalded double it forms the quarter of a circle, and is left open at one side here it may be attatched or loosened at pleasure by strings which are sewed to its sides for the purpose.

To erect this tent, a parsel of ten or twelve poles are provided, fore or five of which are attatched together at one end, they are then elivated and their lower extremities are spread in a circular manner to a width proportionate to the demention of the lodge; in the same position orther poles are leant against those, and the leather is then thrown over them forming a conic figure.

[Lewis] April 9, 1805

When we halted for dinner the squaw busied herself in serching for the wild artichokes which the mice collect and deposit in large hoards. This operation she performed by penetrating the earth with a sharp stick about some small collections of drift wood. Her labour soon proved sucessful, and she procured a good quantity of these roots.

[Lewis] April 13, 1805

The wind was in our favour after 9 a.m. and continued favourable until 3 p.m. We therefore hoisted both the sails in the white perogue, consisting of a small squar sail, and spritsail, which carried her at a pretty good gate, until about 2 in the afternoon when a suddon squall of wind struck us and turned the perogue so much on the side as to allarm Sharbono who was steering at the time. In this state of alarm he threw the perogue with her side to the wind, when the spritsail gibing was as near oversoting the perogue as it was possible to have missed. The wind however abating for an instant I ordered Drewyer to the helm and the sails to be taken in, which was instantly executed and the perogue being steered before the wind was agin plased in a state of security.

This accedent was very near costing us dearly. Beleiving this vessell to be the most steady and safe, we had embarked on board of it our instruments, papers, medicine and the most valuable part of the merchandize which we had still in reserve as presents for the Indians. We had also embarked on board ourselves, with three men who could not swim and the squaw with the young child, all of whom, had the perogue overset, would most probably have perished.

We saw also many tracks of the white bear of enormous size, along the river shore and about the carcases of the buffaloe, on which I presume they feed. We have not as yet seen one of these anamals, tho' their tracks are so abundant and recent. The men as well as ourselves are anxious to meet with some of these bear. The Indians give a very formidable account of the strength and ferocity of this anamal, which they never dare to attack but in parties of six eight or ten persons; and are even then frequently defeated with the loss of one or more of their party.

The savages attack this anamal with their bows and arrows and the indifferent guns with which the traders furnish them. With these they shoot with such uncertainty and at so short a distance, that (unless shot thro' head or heart wound not mortal) they frequently mis their aim & fall a sacrefice to the bear. Two Minetaries were killed during the last winter in an attack on a white bear. This anamall is said more frequently to attack a man on meeting with him, than to flee from him. When the Indians are about to go in quest of the white bear, previous to their departure, they paint themselves and perform all those supersticious rights commonly observed when they are about to make war uppon a neighbouring nation.

[Lewis] April 17, 1805

There were three beaver taken this morning by the party. The men prefer the flesh of this anamal, to that of any other which we have, or are able to procure at this moment. I eat very heartily of the beaver myself, and think it excellent; particularly the tale, and liver.

[Lewis] April 20, 1805

I walked on shore on the &. side of the river . . . in the course of my walk I killed two deer, wounded an elk and a deer; saw the remains of some Indian hunting camps, near which stood a small scaffold of about 7 feet high on which were deposited two doog slays with their harnis. Underneath this scaffold a human body was lying, well rolled in several dressed buffaloe skins and near it a bag of the same materials containing sundry articles belonging to the disceased; consisting of a pare of mockersons, some red and blue earth, beaver's nails, instruments for dressing the buffalo skin, some dryed roots, several platts of the sweet grass, and a small quantity of Mandan tobacco. I presume that the body, as well as the bag containing these articles, had formerly been placed on the scaffold as is the custom of these people, but had fallen down by accedent. Near the scaffold I saw the carcase, of a large dog not yet decayed, which I supposed had been killed at the time the human body was left on the scaffold; this was no doubt the reward, which the poor dog had met with for performing the [blank space in manuscript] friendly office to his mistres of transporting her corps to the place of deposit. It is customary with the Assinniboins, Mandans, Minetares &c. who scaffold their dead, to sacrefice the favorite horses and doggs of their deceased relations, with a view of their being servicable to them in the land of sperits.

[Lewis] April 22, 1805

I asscended to the top of the cutt bluff this morning, from whence I had a most delightfull view of the country, the whole of which except the vally formed by the Missouri is void of timber or underbrush, exposing to the first glance of the spectator immence herds of buffaloe, elk, deer, & antelopes feeding in one common and boundless pasture. We saw a number of bever feeding on the bark of the trees alonge the verge of the river, several of which we shot, found them large and fat. Walking on shore this evening I met with a buffaloe calf which attatched itself to me and continued to follow close at my heels untill I embarked and left it. It appeared allarmed at my dog which was probably the cause of it's so readily attatching itself to me.

[Lewis] April 24, 1805

Soar eyes is a common complaint among the party. I believe it origenates from the immence quantities of sand which is driven by the wind from the sandbars of the river in such clouds that you are unable to discover the opposite bank of the river in many instances. The particles of this sand are so fine and light that they are easily supported by the air, and are carried by the wind for many miles, and at a distance exhibiting every appearance of a collumn of thick smoke. So penetrating is thiss and that we cannot keep any article free from it; in short we are compelled to eat, drink, and breath it very freely. My pocket watch, is out of order, she will run only a few minutes without stoping. I can discover no radical defect in her works, and must therefore attribute it to the sand.

On April 25, the explorers reached the Yellowstone River and camped that night just south of its junction with the Missouri.

[Lewis] April 25, 1805

The water friezed on the oars this morning as the men rowed. . . . My dog had been absent during the last night, and I was fearfull we had lost him altogether. However, much to my satisfaction he joined us at 8 oclock this morning.

Believing that we were no very great distance from the Yellow Stone River, I determined, in order as mush as possible to avoid detention, to proceed by land with a few men to the entrance of that river. . . . When we had proceeded about four miles, I ascended the hills from whence I had a most pleasing view of the country, particularly of the wide and fertile vallies formed by the Missouri and the Yellowstone rivers . . . The buffaloe, elk and antelope are so gentle that we pass near them while feeding, without apearing to excite any alarm among them. . . .

[Lewis] April 26, 1805

This morning I dispatched Joseph Fields up the Yellowstone River with orders to examine it as far as he could conveniently and return the same evening. I walked down and joined the party at their encampment on the point of land formed by the junction of the rivers; found them all in good health, and much pleased at having arrived at this long wished for spot and in order to add in some measure to the general pleasure which seemed to pervade our little community, we ordered a dram to be issued to each person. This soon produced the fiddle, and they spent the evening with much hilarity, singing & dancing, and seemed as perfectly to forget their past toils.

[Lewis] April 29, 1805

I walked on shore with one man. About 8 a.m. fell in with two brown or yellow [white] bear; both of which we wounded; one of them made his escape. The other after my firing on him pursued me seventy or eighty yards, but fortunately had been so badly wounded that he was unable to pursue so closely as to prevent my charging my gun. We again repeated our fire and killed him. It was a male not fully grown. We estimated his weight at 300 lbs not having the means of ascertaining it precisely. . . .

These are all the particulars in which this anamal appeared to me to differ from the black bear. It is a much more furious and formidable anamal, and will frequently pursue the hunter when wounded. It is astonishing to see the wounds they will bear before they can be put to death. The Indians may well fear this anamal equiped as they generally are with their bows and arrows or indifferent fuzees, but in the hands of skillfull riflemen they are by no means as formidable or dangerous as they have been represented.

[Lewis] May 3, 1805

The morning being very could we did not set out as early as usual; ice formed on a kettle of water ¼ inch thick. . . . After dinner Capt. Clark pursued his walk, which I continued with the party, it being a rule which we had established, never to be absent at the same time from the party. . . . We saw vast quantities of buffaloe, elk, deer principally of the long tale kind, antelope or goats, beaver, geese, ducks, brant and some swan. We saw an unusual number of porcupines from which we determined to call the river after that anamal, and accordingly denominated it Porcupine River.[22] I walked out a little distance and met with 2 porcupines which were feeding on the young willow which grow in great abundance on all the sandbars; this anamal is exceedingly clumsy and not very watchfull. I approached so near one of them before it percieved me that I touched it with my espontoon.

[Clark] May 5, 1805

In the evening we saw a brown or grisley beare on a sand beech. I went out with one man Geo Drewyer & killed the bear, which was verry large and a turrible looking animal, which we found verry hard to kill. We shot ten balls into him before we killed him, & 5 of those balls through his lights. This animal is the largest of the carnivorous kind I ever saw. We had nothing that could way him. I think his weight may be stated at 500 pounds.

---

1. The last sentence appears only in Clark's field notes. —LYJ
2. Corruption of *blaireau*, a French name of the badger. The Pawnee word is *cuhkatus*. —Ed.
3. It was a coyote, *Canis latrans*, one of the most familiar animals of the West but little known to the explorers. —Ed.
4. It is now believed that Floyd died of a ruptured appendix and consequent peritonitis. Moulton points out that the ailment was not even recognized by medical science until twenty years after the expedition, and the first successful surgical treatment came in 1884. —LYJ
5. This was the first bison killed by a member of the party. —LYJ

6. Pierre Dorion Sr., a French fur trader who had met the captains on the river in June. They persuaded him to join them as an interpreter to assist their negotiations with the Yanktons. —Ed.

7. The prairie-dog, then unknown to scientists. —Ed.

8. These "goats" were antelopes, or pronghorns, new to science when discovered by Lewis and Clark in 1804. They were not technically named until 1815.

9. Prairie-dogs.

10. Private George Shannon, the youngest member of the party, had become lost while hunting back on August 26.

11. The northern jack-rabbit.

12. This is Lewis's last journal entry of the year. As Stephen Ambrose writes in *Undaunted Courage*, "Either Lewis put down his quill, not to take it up again until April 1805—or what he wrote is lost." —LYJ

13. *Bois roule*, literally "rolled wood"—a mixture of tobacco with scrapings or shavings from various woods, especially that of sumac, red osier, and other bogwoods and bearberry. —Ed.

14. A "port fire" is a fuse used to ignite the touchhole of a cannon. —LYJ

15. In his 1814 edition, Biddle writes: "By way of amusement he told them that he had once been a wild animal and was caught and tamed by his master, and to convince them showed them feats of strength which added to his looks made him more terrible than we wished him to be." —LYJ

16. Biddle says that the Arikaras regarded such intercourse with strangers as disgraceful, when it occurred without the husband's or brother's consent. —Ed.

17. This was the expedition's first encounter with a grizzly. Moutton notes that Lewis's natural history note and weather remarks for this date show that Pierre Cruzatte shot the ani-

mal and had to beat such a hasty retreat that he left his gun behind. —LYJ

18. Fort Mandan, the wintering place of the expedition, was located on the east bank of the Missouri, seven or eight miles below the mouth of Knife River; it was nearly opposite the site of the later Fort Clark.

19. This is Toussaint Charbonneau, husband of Sacagawea, a French-Canadian fur trader who had been living with the Hidatsas for several years.

20. From this point to the thirteenth of February, the journal is written by Lewis, during Clark's absence on a hunting expedition (February 4–12). This is the only hiatus in Clark's regular journalizing throughout the entire expedition. —Ed.

21. This was Sacagawea. The child was Jean-Baptiste Charbonneau ("Pomp").

22. Now Poplar River; the name Porcupine is in our day applied to a branch of Milk River. —Ed.

VOLUME TWO

From Two-Thousand-Mile Creek to Shoshoni Camp on Lemhi River

May 6, 1805–August 20, 1805

[Lewis] May 9, 1805

Capt. C. killed 2 bucks and 2 buffaloes. I also killed one buffaloe . . . we saved the best of the meat, and from the cow I killed we saved the necessary materials for making what our wrighthand cook Charbono calls the *boudin (poudingue) blanc*, and immediately set him about preparing them for supper.

This white pudding we all esteem one of the greatest delicacies of the forrest. It may not be amiss therefore to give it a place. About 6 feet of the lower extremity of the large gut of the buffaloe is the first morsel that the cook makes love to. This he holds fast at one end with the right hand, while with the forefinger and thumb of the left he gently compresses it, and discharges what be says *is not good to eat*, but of which in the sequel we get a moderate portion. The mustle lying underneath the shoulder blade next to the back, and fillets are next saught, these are needed up very fine with a good portion of kidney suit [suet]; to this composition is then added a just proportion of pepper and salt and a small quantity of flour.

Thus far advanced, our skilfull opporater [Charbonneau] seizes his receptacle, which has never once touched the water, for that would intirely distroy the regular order of the whole procedure. You will not forget that the side you now see is that covered with a good coat of fat provided the anamal be in good order. The operator sceizes the receptacle, I say, and tying it fast at one end turns it inward and begins now with repeated evolutions of the hand and arm, and a brisk motion of the finger and thumb to put in what he says is *bon pour manger*; thus by stuffing and compressing he soon distends the receptacle to the utmost limmits of its power of expansion, and in the course of it's longtudinal progress it drives from the other end of the receptacle a much larger portion of the [blank space in manuscript] than was previously discharged by the finger and thumb of the left hand in a former part of the operation. Thus when the sides of the receptacle are skilfully exchanged the outer for the iner, and all is compleatly filled with something good to eat, it is tyed at the other end, but not any cut off, for that would make the pattern too scant.

It is then baptised in the Missouri with two dips and a flirt, and bobbed into the kettle; from whence, after it be well boiled it is fryed with bears oil untill it becomes brown, when taken and it is ready to esswage the pangs of a keen appetite or such as travelers in the wilderness are seldom at a loss for.

[Lewis] May 11, 1805

About 5 P.M. my attention was struck by one of the party runing at a distance towards us and making signs and hollowing as if in distress. I ordered the perogues to put too, and waited untill he arrived. I now found that it was Bratton the man with the soar hand whom I had permitted to walk on shore. He arrived so much out of breath that it was several minutes before he could tell what had happened. At length he informed me that in the woody bottom about 1½[miles] below us he had shot a brown bear which iminediately turned on him and pursued him a considerable distance but he had wounded it so badly that it could not overtake him.

I immediately turned out with seven of the party in quest of this monster. We at length found his trale and persued him about a mile by the blood through very thick brush of rosbushes and the large leafed willow; we finally found him concealed in some very thick brush and shot him through the skull with two balls; we proceeded [to] dress him as soon possible. We found him in good order; it was a monstrous beast, not quite so large as that we killed a few days past but in all other rispects much the same . . . we now found that Bratton had shot him through the center of the lungs, notwithstanding which he had pursued him near half a mile and had returned more than double that distance and with his tallons had prepared himself a bed the earth of about 2 feet deep and five long and was perfectly alive when we found him which could not have been less than 2 hours after he received the wound.

These bear being so hard to die reather intimedates us all. I must confess I do not like the gentlemen and had reather fight two Indians than one bear.

[Lewis] May 14, 1805

In the evening the men in two of the rear canoes discovered a large brown bear lying in the open grounds about 300 paces from the river, and six of them went out to attack him, all good hunters. They took the advantage of a small eminence which concealed them and got within 40 paces of him unperceived. Two of them reserved their fires as had been previously conscerted. The four others fired nearly at the same time and put each his bullet through him. Two of the balls passed through the bulk of both lobes of his lungs.

In an instant this monster ran at them with open mouth, the two who had reserved their fires discharged their pieces at him as he came towards them. Boath of them struck him, one only slightly and the other fortunately broke his shoulder. This however only retarded his motion for a moment only. The men unable to reload their guns took to flight, the bear pursued and had very nearly overtaken them before they reached the river.

Two of the party betook themselves to a canoe and the others separated and concealed themselves among the willows, reloaded their pieces, each discharged his piece at him as they had an opportunity they struck him several times again but the guns served only to direct the bear to them. In this manner he pursued two of them seperately so close that they were obliged to throw aside their guns and pouches and throw themselves into the river altho' the bank was nearly twenty feet perpendicular. So enraged was this anamal that he plunged into the river only a few feet behind the second man he had compelled [to] take refuge in the water, when one of those who still remained on shore shot him through the head and finally killed him.

It was after the sun had set before these men come up with us, where we had been halted by an occurrence, which I have now to recappitulate, and which altho' happily passed without ruinous injury, I cannot recollect but with the utmost trepidation and horror. This is the upseting and narrow escape of the white perogue. It happened unfortunately for us this evening that Charbono was at the helm of this perogue, in stead of Drewyer, who had previously steered her. Charbono cannot swim and is perhaps the most timid waterman in the world. Perhaps it was equally unluckey that Capt. C. and myself were both on shore at that moment, a circumstance which rarely happened; and tho' we were on the shore opposite to the perogue, were too far distant to be heard or to do more than remain spectators of her fate. In this perogue were embarked, our papers, instruments, books medicine, a great part of our merchandise and in short almost every article indispensably necessary to further the views, or insure the success of the enterprise in which we are now launched to the distance of 2200 miles.

Surfice it to say, that the perogue was under sail when a sudon squawl of wind struck her obliquely, and turned her considerably, the steersman allarmed, in stead of putting her before the wind, lufted her up into it. The wind was so violent that it drew the brace of the squarsail out of the hand of the man who was attending it, and instantly upset the perogue and would have turned her completely topsaturva had it not have been from the resistance made by the oarning [awning] against the water.

In this situation Capt. C. and myself both fired our guns to attract the attention if possible of the crew and ordered the halyards to be cut and the sail hawled in, but they did not hear us. Such was their confusion and consternation at this moment that they suffered the perogue to lye on her side for half a minute before they took the sail in. The perogue then wrighted but had filled within an inch of the gunwals.

Charbono still crying to his god for mercy had not yet recollected the rudder, nor could the repeated orders of the bowsman, Cruzat, bring him to his recollection untill he threatend to shoot him instantly if he did not take hold of the rudder and do his duty. The waves by this time were runing, very high, but the fortitude resolution and good conduct of Cruzat saved her. He ordered 2 of the men to throw out the water with some kettles that fortunately were convenient, while himself and two others rowed her as[h]ore.

After having all matters arranged for the evening as well as the nature of circumstances would permit, we thought it a proper occasion to console ourselves and cheer the sperits of our men and accordingly took a drink of grog and gave each man a gill of sperits.

[Lewis] May 16, 1805

By 4 oClock in the evening our instruments, medicine, merchandise provision &c., were perfectly dryed, repacked and put on board the perogue. The loss we sustained was not so great as we had at first apprehended. Our medicine sustained the greatest injury, several articles of which were intirely spoiled, and many others considerably injured. The ballance of our losses consisted of some gardin seeds, a small quantity of gunpowder, and a few culinary articles which fell overboard and sunk. The Indian woman to whom I ascribe equal fortitude and resolution, with any person onboard at the time of the accedent, caught and preserved most of the light articles which were washed overboard . . .

The early part of the day two of our men fired on a panther, a little below our encampment, and wounded it; they informed us that it was very large, had just killed a deer partly devoured it, and in the act of concealing the ballance as they discovered him. . . . This morning a white bear toar Labuiche's coat which he had left in the plains.

[Lewis] May 17, 1805

We were roused late at night by the sergt. of the guard, and warned of the danger we were in from a large tree that had taken fire and which leant immediately over our lodge. We had the loge removed, and a few minutes after a large proportion of the top of the tree fell on the place the lodge had stood; had we been a few minutes later we should have been crushed to attoms.

[Lewis] May 19, 1805

One of the party wounded a beaver, and my dog as usual swam in to catch it. The beaver bit him through the hind leg and cut the artery; it was with great difficulty that I could stop the blood; I fear it will yet prove fatal to him.

[Lewis] May 20, 1805

About five miles abe (*above*) the mouth of the [Muscle Shell] river a handsome river of about fifty yards in width discharged itself into the shell river . . . this stream we called Sah-ca-ger we-ah (*Sah-ca-gah-we-a*) or bird woman's river, after our interpreter the snake woman.

[Clark] May 25, 1805

I walked on shore and killed a female *ibi* or big horn animal. In my absence Drewyer & Bratten killed two others. This animal is a species peculiar to this upper part of the Missouri. . . . It was somewhat larger than the mail of the common deer; the body reather thicker deeper and not so long in proportion to it's hight as the common deer; the head and horns of the male are remarkably large compared with the other parts of the animal . . . the horn is of a light brown colour; when dressed it is almost white extreamly transparent and very elastic. This horn is used by the natives in constructing their bows; I have no doubt of it's elegance and usefullness in hair combs, and might probably answer as maney valuable purpoces to civilized man, as it does to the native indians, who form their water cups, spoons and platters of it. . . .

The places they generally collect to lodge is the cranies or crevices of the rocks in the face of inaccessable precepices, where the wolf nor bear can reach them, and where indeed man himself would in maney instances find a similar deficiency; yet those animals bound from rock to rock and stand apparently in the most careless manner on the side of precipices of maney hundred feet.

On arriving to the summit [of] one of the highest points in the neighbourhood I thought myself well repaid for my labour; as from this point I beheld the Rocky Mountains for the first time . . . these points of the Rocky Mountains were covered with snow and the sun shone on it in such manner as to give me the most plain and satisfactory view.

While I viewed these mountains I felt a secret pleasure in finding myself so near the head of the heretofore conceived boundless Missouri; but when I reflected on the difficulties which this snowey barrier would most probably throw in my way to the Pacific, and the sufferings and hardships of myself and party in thim, it in some measure counter ballanced the joy I had felt in the first moments in which I gazed on them. But as I have always held it a crime to anticipate evils I will believe it a good comfortable road untill I am compelled to believe differently. . . .

On my return to camp I trod within [a] few inches of a rattle snake but being in motion I passed before he could probably put himself in a striking attitude and fortunately escaped his bite. I struck about with my espontoon being directed in some measure by his nois untill I killed him.

Last night we were all allarmed by a large buffaloe bull, which swam over from the opposite shore and coming along side of the white perogue, climbed over it to land. He then allarmed ran up the bank in full speed directly towards the fires, and was within 18 inches of the heads of some of the men who lay sleeping before the centinel could allarm him or make him change his course. Still more alarmed, he now took his direction immediately towards our lodge, passing between 4 fires and within a few inches of the heads of one range of the men as they yet lay sleeping. When he came near the tent, my dog saved us by causing him to change his course a second time, which he did by turning a little to the right, and was quickly out of sight, leaving us by this time all in an uproar with our guns in o[u]r hands, enquiring of each other the ca[u]se of the alarm.

The next morning we found that the buffaloe in passing the perogue had trodden on a rifle, which belonged to Capt. Clark's black man, who had negligently left her in the perogue.

This morning we set out at an early hour . . . passed a handsome river. . . . Cap. C. who assended this R. much higher than I did has thought proper to call (called) it *Judieths* River. . . .¹

I counted the remains of the fires of 126 Indian lodges which appeared to be of very recent date perhaps 12 or 15 days. Capt. Clark also saw a large encampment just above the entrance of this river on the star' side of reather older date, probably they were the same Indians.

The Indian woman with us examined the mockersons which we found at these encampments and informed us that they were not of her nation the snake Indians, but she beleived they were some of the Indians who inhabit the country on this side of [the] Rocky Mountains and North of the Missoury and I think it most probable that they were the Minetaries of Fort de Prarie.

Today we passed on the star' side the remains of a vast many mangled carcases of buffalow which had been driven over a precipice of 120 feet by the Indians and perished. The water appeared to have washed away a part of this immence pile of slaughter and still their remained the fragments of at least a hundred carcases. They created a most horrid stench. In this manner the Indians of the Missouri distroy vast herds of buffaloe at a stroke.

For this purpose one of the most active and fleet young men is scelected and disguised in a robe of buffaloe skin, having also the skin of the buffaloe's head with the years and horns fastened on his head in form of a cap. Thus caparisoned he places himself at a convenient distance between a herd of buffaloe and a precipice proper for the purpose, which happens in many places on this river for miles together. The other indians now surround the herd on the back and flanks and at a signal agreed on all shew themselves at the same time moving forward towards the buffaloe. The disguised Indian or decoy has taken care to place himself sufficiently nigh the buffaloe to be noticed by them when they take to flight and runing before them they follow him in full speede to the precipice.

The cattle behind driving those in front over and seeing them go do not look or hesitate about following untill the whole are precipitated down the precepice forming one common mass of dead an[d] mangled carcases. The decoy in the mean time has taken care to secure himself in some cranney or crivice of the clift which he had previously prepared for that purpose. The part of the decoy I am informed is extreamly dangerous. If they are not very fleet runers the buffaloe tread them under foot and crush them to death, and sometimes drive them over the precipice.

[Lewis] May 30, 1805

The obstructions of rocky points and riffles still continue as yesterday; at those places the men are compelled to be in the water even to their armpits, and the water is yet very could, and so frequent are those points that they are one fourth of their time in the water. Added to this the banks and bluffs along which they are obliged to pass are so slippery and the mud so tenacious that they are unable to wear their mockersons, and in that situation draging the heavy burthen of a canoe and walking acasionally for several hundred yards over the sharp fragments of rocks which tumble from the clifts and garnish the borders of the river; in short their labour is incredibly painfull and great, yet those faithfull fellows bear it without a murmur.

The toe rope of the white perogue, the only one indeed of hemp, and that on which we most depended, gave way today at a bad point. The perogue swung and but slightly touched a rock; yet was very near oversetting; I fear her evil gennii will play so many pranks with her that she will go to the bottom some of those days . . .

The hills and river clifts which we passed today exhibit a most romantic appearance. The bluffs of the river rise to the hight of from 2 to 300 feet and in most places nearly perpendicular; they are formed of remarkable white sandstone which is sufficiently soft to give way readily to the impression of water. . . . The water in the course of time in decending from those hills and plains on either side of the river has trickled down the soft sand clifts and woarn it into a thousand grotesque figures, which with the help of a little immagination and an oblique view, at a distance are made to represent eligant ranges of lofty freestone buildings, having their parapets well stocked with statuary; collumns of various sculpture both grooved and plain, are also seen supporting long galleries in front of those buildings; in other places on a much nearer approach and with the help of less immagination we see the remains or ruins of eligant buildings; some collumns standing and almost entire with their pedestals and capitals; others retaining their pedestals but deprived by time or accident of their capitals, some lying prostrate and broken, others in the form of vast pyramids of connic structure bearing a serees of other pyramids on their tops becoming less as they ascend and finally terminating in a sharp point. Nitches and alcoves of various forms and sizes are seen at different hights as we pass. . . .

As we passed on it seemed as if those seens of visionary inchantment would never have and [an] end; for here it is too that nature presents to the view of the traveler vast ranges of walls of tolerable workmanship, so perfect indeed are those walls that I should have thought that nature had attempted here to rival the human art of masonry had I not recollected that she had first began her work.

I saw near those bluffs the most beautifull fox that I ever beheld. The colours appeared to me to be a fine orrange yellow, white and black. I endevoured to kill this anamal but it discovered me at a considerable distance and finding that I could get no nearer, I fired on him as he ran, and missed him; he concealed himself under the rocks of the clift. It appeared to me to be about the size of the common red fox of the Atlantic states, or reather smaller than the large fox common to this country; convinced I am that it is a distinct species.[2]

[Lewis] June 3, 1805

This morning early we passed over and formed a camp on the point formed by the junction of the two large rivers. . . . An interesting question was now to be determined; which of these rivers was the Missouri, or that river which the Minnetares call *Amahte Arzzha* or Missouri, and which they had described to us as approaching very near to the Columbia River. To mistake the stream at this period of the season, two months of the traveling season having now elapsed, and to ascend such stream to the rocky mountain or perhaps much further before we could inform ourselves whether it did approach the Columbia or not, and then be obliged to return and take the other stream would not only loose us the whole of this season but would probably so dishearten the party that it might defeat the expedition altogether.

Convinced we were that the utmost circumspection and caution was necessary in deciding on the stream to be taken. To this end an investigation of both streams was the first thing to be done; to learn their widths, debths, comparitive rappidity of their courants and thence the comparitive bodies of water furnished by each. Accordingly we dispatched two light canoes with three men in each up those streams; we also sent out several small parties by land with instructions to penetrate the country as far as they conveniently can permitting themselves time to return this evening and indeavour if possible to discover the distant bearing of those rivers by ascending the rising grounds.

Between the time of a.m. and meridian Capt. C. & myself stroled out to the top of the hights in the fork of these rivers from whence we had an extensive and most enchanting view; the country in every detection around us was one vast plain in which innumerable herds of buffalow were seen attended by their shepperds the wolves; the solatary antelope which now had their young were distributed over it's face; some herds of elk were also seen. The verdure perfectly cloathed the ground, the weather was pleasent and fair; to the south we saw a range of lofty mountains which we supposed to be a continuation of the S. mountains . . . behind these mountains and at a great distance, a second and more lofty range of mountains appeared to strech across the country in the same direction with the others, reaching from West, to the N. of N.W., where their snowey tops lost themselves beneath the horizon. This last range was perfectly covered with snow. . . . The choke cherry grows here in abundance both in the river bottoms and in the steep ravenes along the river bluffs. Saw the yellow and red courants, not yet ripe; also the goosberry which begins to ripen; the wild rose which grows here in great abundance in the bottoms of all these rivers is now in full bloom, and adds not a little to the beauty of the cenery.

We took the width of the two rivers, found the left hand or S. fork 372 yards and the N. fork 200. The north fork is deeper than the other but it's courant not so swift; it's waters run in the same boiling and roling manner which has uniformly characterized the Missouri throughout it's whole course so far; it's waters are of a whitish brown colour very thick and terbid, also characteristic of the Missouri; while the south fork is perfectly transparent runs very rappid but with a smoth unriffled surface it's bottom composed of round and flat smooth stones like most rivers issuing from a mountainous country. The bed of the N. fork composed of some gravel but principally mud. In short the air & character of this river is so precisely that of the Missouri below that the party with very few exceptions have already pronounced the N. fork to be the Missouri.

Myself and Capt C. not quite so precipitate. Have not yet decided but if we were to give our opinions I believe we should be in the minority, certain it is that the north fork gives the colouring matter and character which is retained from hence to the gulph of Mexico. I am confident that this river rises in and passes a great distance through an open plain country. I expect that it has some of it's sou[r]ces on the eastern side of the rocky mountain south of the Saskashawan but that it dose not penetrate the first range of these mountains and that much the greater part of it's sources are in a northwardly direction towards the lower and middle parts of the Saskashawan in the open plains. Convinced I am that if it penetrated the Rocky Mountains to any great distance it's waters would be clearer unless it should run an immence distance indeed after leaving those mountains through these level plains in order to acquire it's turbid hue.

What astonishes us a little is that the Indians who appeared to be so well acquainted with the geography of this country should not have mentioned this river on wright hand if it be not the Missouri; *the river that scolds at all others*, as they call it if there is in reallity such an one, ought agreeably to their account, to have fallen in a considerable distance below, and on the other hand if this right hand or N. fork be the Missouri. I am equally astonished at their not mentioning the S. fork which they must have passed in order to get to those large falls which they mention on the Missouri. . . .

Capt. Clark and myself concluded to set out early the next morning with a small party each, and ascend these rivers untill we could perfectly satisfy ourselves of the one, which it would be most expedi-

ent for us to take on our main journey to the Pacific. Accordingly it
was agreed that I should ascend the right hand fork, and he the left.

[Lewis] June 5, 1805

We saw one of the largest collection of the burrowing or barking
squirrels that we had ever yet seen; we passed through a skirt of the
territory of this community for about 7 miles. . . . As we had not
killed or eat anything today we each killed a burrowing squirrel as
we passed them in order to make shure of our suppers. . . . I had their
burrowing squirrels roasted by way of experiment and found the
flesh well flavored and tender; some of them were very fat.

[Lewis] June 6, 1805

I now became well convinced that this branch of the Missouri
had it's direction too much to the north for our rout to the Pacific,
and therefor determined to return the next day. . . .

[Lewis] June 7, 1805

It continued to rain almost without intermission last night and
as I expected we had a most disagreable and wrestless night. Our
camp possessing no allurements, we left our watery beads at an
early hour and continued our rout down the river . . . the grownd
remarkably slipry, insomuch that we were unable to walk on the
sides of the bluffs where we had passed as we ascended the river.
Notwithstanding the rain that has now fallen the earth of these
bluffs is not wet to a greater debth than 2 inches; in it's present
state it is precisely like walking over frozan grownd which is
thawed to small debth and slips equally as bad. . . . In passing
along the face of one of these bluffs today I sliped at a narrow pass
of about 30 yards in length and but for a quick and fortunate
recovery by means of my espontoon I should been precipitated into
the river down a craggy precipice of about ninety feet.

I had scarcely reached a place on which I could stand with tolerable safety even with the assistance of my espontoon before I heard a voice behind me cry out God, god Capt., what shall I do? On turning about I found it was Windsor who had sliped and fallen about the center of this narrow pass and was lying prostrate on his belley, with his wright hand arm and leg over the precipice while he was holding on the with left arm and foot as well as he could which appeared to be with much difficulty.

I discovered his danger and the trepedation which he was in gave me still futher concern for I expected every instant to see hin loose his strength and slip off. Altho' much allarmed at his situation I disguised my feelings and spoke very calmly to him and assured him that he was in no kind of danger, to take the knife out of his belt behind him with his wright hand and dig a whole with it in the face of the bank to receive his wright foot which he did and then raised himself to his knees; I then directed him to take off his mockersons and to come forward on his hands and knees holding the knife in one hand and the gun in the other. This he happily effected and escaped.

Wĕ continued our disagreeable march through the rain mud and water . . . and encamped in an old Indian stick lodge which afforded us a dry and comfortable shelter . . . we roasted and eat a hearty supper of our venison not having taisted a morsel before during the day. I now laid myself down on some willow bought to a comfortable nights rest, and felt indeed as if I was fully repaid for the toil and pain of the day, so much so will a good shelter, a dry bed, and comfortable supper revive the sperits of the wearyed, wet and hungry traveler.

[Lewis] June 8, 1805

The whole of my party to a man except myself were fully persuaided that this river was the Missouri, but being fully of opinion that it was neither the main stream, nor that which it would be advisable for us to take, I determined to give it a name and in honour of Miss Maria W—d.[3] Called it Maria's River. It is true that the hue of the waters of this turbulent and troubled stream but illy comport with the pure celestial virtues and amiable qualifications of that lovely fair one.

[Lewis] June 9, 1805

Today we examined our maps . . . and fully settled in our minds the propryety of addopting the south fork for the Missouri. . . . The Indian information also argued strongly in favor of the south fork. They informed us that the water of the Missouri was nearly transparent at the great falls. This is the case with the water of the south fork . . . those ideas as they occurred to me I indevoured to impress on the minds of the party all of whom except Capt. C. being still firm in the belief that the N. fork was the Missouri and that which we ought to take. They said very cheerfully that they were ready to follow us any wher[e] we thought proper to direct but that they still thought that the other was the river and that they were affiraid that the south fork would soon termineate in the mountains and leave us at a great distance from the Columbia.

Cruzatte who had been an old Missouri navigator and who from his integrity knowledge and skill as a waterman had acquired the confidence of every individual of the party declared it as his opinion that the N. fork was the true genuine Missouri and could be no other.

Finding them so determined in this beleif, and wishing that it we were in an error to be able to detect it and rectify it as soon as possible it was agreed between Capt. Clark and myself that one of us should set out with a small party by land up the south fork and continue our route up it until we found the falls or reached the snowy mountains . . . which should . . . determine this question prety accurately.

In the evening Cruzatte gave us some music on the violin and the men passed the evening in dancing singing &c. and were extreemly cheerfull.

[Lewis] June 10, 1805

I still feel myself somewhat unwell with the disentary, but determined to set out in the morning up to south fork or Missouri leaving Capt. Clark to . . . follow me by water with the party; accordingly gave orders to Drewyer, Joseph Fields, Givson and Goodrigh to hold themselves in readiness to accompany me in the morning. *Sah-câh-gâh, we â* our Indian woman is very sick this evening. Capt. C. bled her.

[Lewis] June 12, 1805

We passed a ridge of land considerably higher than the adjacent plain. On either side, from thie hight we had a most beautifull and piuresk view of the Rocky Mountains which wer perfectly covered with snow . . . they appear to be formed of server ranged esch succeeding range rising higher than the preceding one untill the most distant appear to loose their snowey tops in the clouds. This was an august spectacle and still rendered more formidable by the recollection that we had them to pass.

[Clark] June 12, 1805

The enterpreters wife verry *sick* so much that I move her into the back part of our covered part of the perogue which is cool, her own situation being a verry hot one in the bottom of the perogue exposed to the sun.

[Lewis] June 13, 1805

From the extremity of this roling country I overlooked a most beatifull and level plain of great extent or at least 50 or sixty miles.

In this there were infinitely more buffaloe than I had ever before witnessed at a view. . . . I sent Fields on my right and Drewyer and Gibson on my left with orders to kill some meat and join me at the river where I should halt for dinner.

I had proceded on this course about two miles with Goodrich at some distance behind me whin my ears were saluted with the agreeable sound of a fall of water and advancing a little further I saw the spray arrise above the plain like a collumn of smoke which would frequently dispear again in an instant caused I presume by the wind which blew pretty hard from the S.W. I did not however loose my direction to this point which soon began to make a roaring too tremendious to be mistaken for any cause short of the great falls of the Missouri.

I hurryed down the hill which was about 200 feet high and difficult of access, to gaze on this sublimely grand spectacle. I took my position on the top of some rocks about 20 feet high opposite the center of the falls. This chain of rocks appear once to have formed a part of those over which the waters tumbled, but in the course of time has been seperated from it to the distance of 150 yards lying prarrallel to it and a butment against which the water after falling over the precipice beats with great fury. This barrier extends on the right to the perpendicular clift which forms that board [border] of the river, but to the distance of 120 yards next to the clift it is but a few feet above the level of the water, and here the water in very high tides appears to pass in a channel of 40 yds. next to & higher part of the ledg of rocks; on the left it extends within 80 or ninty yards of the clift which is also perpendicular; between this abrupt extremity of the ledge of rocks and the perpendicular bluff the whole body of water passes with incredible swiftness. Immediately at the cascade the river is about 300 yds. wide; about ninty or a hundred yards of this next the lard. bluff is a smoth even sheet of water falling over a precipice of at least eighty feet. The remaining

part of about 200 yards on my right formes the grandest sight I
ever beheld.

The hight of the fall is the same of the other but the irregular
and somewhat projecting rocks below receives the water in it's passage down and brakes it into a perfect white foam which assumes a
thousand forms in a moment sometimes flying up in jets of
sparkling foam to the hight of fifteen or twenty feet and are
scarcely formed before large roling bodies of the same beaten and
foaming water is thrown over and conceals them.

In short the rocks seem to be most happily fixed to present a
sheet of the whitest beaten froath for 200 yards in length and about
80 feet perpendicular. The water after decending strikes against
the butment before mentioned or that on which I stand and seems
to reverberate and being met by the more impetuous courant they
roll and swell into half formed billows of great hight which rise
and again disappear in an instant.

This butment of rock defends a handsome little bottom of
about three acres which is deversified and agreeably shaded with
some cottonwood trees; in the lower extremity of the bottom there
is a very thick grove of the same kind of trees which are small, in
this wood there are several Indian lodges formed of sticks.

From the reflection of the sun on the sprev or mist which arrises
from these falls there is a beatifull rainbow produzed which adds
not a little to the beauty of this majestically grand senery.

After weighting this imperfect description I again viewed the
falls and was so much disgusted with the imperfect idea which it
conveyed of the scene that I determined to draw my pen across it
and begin agin, but then reflected that I could not perhaps succeed
better than pening the first impressions of the mind. I wished for
the pencil of Salvator Rosa or the pen of Thompson[4] that I might
be enabled to give to the enlightened world some just idea of this
truly magnifficent and sublimely grand object, which has from the

commencement of time been concealed from the view of civilized man; but this was fruitless and vain.

I most sincerely regreted that I had not brought a crimee [camera] obscura with me by the assistance of which even I could have hoped to have done better but alas this was also out of my reach; I therefore with the assistance of my pen only indeavoured to trace some of the stronger features of this seen by the assistance of which and my recollection aided by some able pencil I hope still to give to the world some faint idea of an object which at this moment fills me with such pleasure and astonishment; and which of it's kind I will venture to ascert is second to but one in the known world.

On my return I found the party at camp; they had butchered the buffaloe and brought in some more meat as I had directed. Goodrich had caught half a douzen very fine trout.[5] . . . My fare is really sumptuous this evening; buffaloe's humps, tongues and marrowbones, fine trout parched meal pepper and salt, and a good appetite; the last is not considered the least of the luxuries.

[Lewis] June 14, 1805

I took my gun and espontoon and thought I would walk a few miles and see where the rappids termineated above, and return to dinner. . . . After passing one continued rappid and three small cascades of about for or five feet at the distance of about five miles I arrived at a fall of about 19 feet . . . I should have returned from hence but hearing a tremendious roaring above me I continued my rout across the point of a hill a few hundred yards further and was again presented by one of the most beatifull objects in nature, a cascade of about fifty feet perpendicular streching at right angles across the river from side to side to the distance of at least a quarter of a mile. Here the river pitches over a shelving rock, with an edge as regular and as streight as if formed by art, without a nich or brake in it. The water decends in one even and interupted sheet to the bottom where dashing against the rocky bottom [it] rises into foaming billows of great hight and rappidly glides away, hising flashing and sparkling as it departs. The sprey rises from one extremity to the other to 50 f. I now thought that if a skillfull painter had been asked to make a beautifull cascade that he would most probably have presented the precise immage of this one. Nor could I for some time determine on which of those two great cataracts to bestoe the palm, on this or that when I had discovered yesterday; at length I determined between these two rivals for glory that this was *pleasingly beautifull*, while the other was *sublimely grand*.

I had scarcely infixed my eyes from this pleasing object before I discovered another fall above at the distance of half a mile. . . . I found this to be a cascade of about 14 feet possessing a perpendicular pitch of about 6 feet . . . in any other neighbourhood but this, such a cascade would probably be extoled for it's bea[u]ty and magnifficence, but here I passed it by with but little attention. . . . At the distance of 2 ½ miles I arrived at another cataract of 26 feet. . . . This fall is certainly much the greatest I ever behald except those two which I have mentioned below. It is incomparably a greater cataract and a more noble interesting object that the celibrated falls of the Potomac of Sookiln [Schuylkill] &c. . . .

I therefore determined to ascend the hill behind me which promised a fine prospect of the adjacent country, nor was I disappointed on my arrival at it's summit. From hence I overlooked a most beautifull and extensive plain reaching from the river to the base of the snowclad mountains to the S. and S. west. I also observed the missoury streching it's meandering course to the south through this plain. . . . In these plains and more particularly in the valley just below me immence herds of buffaloe are feeding. The Missouri just above this hill makes a bend to the south where it lies a smoth even and unruffled sheet of water of nearly amile in width bearing on its waty bosome vast flocks of geese which feed at pleasure in the delightfull pasture on either border. . . .

I scelected a fat buffaloe and shot him very well, through the lungs. While I was gazeing attentively on the poor anarmal discharging blood in streams from his mouth and nostrils, expecting him to fall every instant, and having entirely forgotten to reload my rifle, a large white, or reather brown bear, had perceived and crept on me within 20 steps before I discovered him.

In the first moment I drew up my gun to shoot, but at the same instant recolected that she was not loaded and that he was too near for me to hope to perform this opperation before he reached me, as he was then briskly advancing on me. It was an open level plain, not a bush within miles nor a tree within less than three hundred yards of me; the river bank was sloping and not more than three feet above the level of the water. In short there was no place by means of which I could conceal myself from this monster until I could charge my rifle; in this situation I thought of retreating in a brisk walk as fast as he was advancing untill I could reach a tree about 300 yards below me, but I had no sooner terned myself about but he pitched at me, open mouthed and full speed.

I ran about 80 yards and found he gained on me fast. I then run into the water. The idea struck me to get into the water to such debth that I could stand and he would be obliged to swim, and that I could in that situation defend myself with my espontoon. Accordingly I ran haistily into the water about waist deep, and faced about and presented the point of my espontoon.

At this instant he arrived at the edge of the water within about 20 feet of me; the moment I put myself in this attitude of defence he sudonly wheeled about as if frightened, declined the combat on such unequal grounds, and retreated with quite as great precipitation as he had just before pursued me. As soon as I saw him run off in that manner I returned to the shore and charged my gun, which I had still retained in my hand throughout this curious adventure. I saw him run through the level open plain about three miles, till he disappeared in the woods on Medecine River; during the whole of this distance he ran at full speed, sometimes appearing to look behind him as if he expected pursuit.

I now began to reflect on this novil occurrence and indeavoured to account for this sudden retreat of the bear. I at first thought that perhaps he had not smelt me bofore he arrived at the waters edge so near me, but I then reflected that he had pursued me for about 80 or 90 yards before I took [to] the water and on examination saw the grownd toarn with his tallons immediately on the impression of my steps; and the cause of his allarm still remains with misterious and unaccountable. So it was and I felt myself not a little gratifyed that he had declined the combat.

I now determined to return having by my estimate about 12 miles to walk. I looked at my watch and found it was half after six p.m. in returning through the level bottom of Medecine River and about 200 yards distant from the Missouri, my direction led me directly to an anamal that I at first supposed was a wolf; but on nearer approach or about sixty paces distant I discovered that it was not. It's colour was a brownish yellow; it was standing near it's burrow, and when I approached it thus nearly, it couched itself down like a cat looking immediately at me as if it designed to spring on me.

I took aim at it and fired. It instantly disappeared in it's burrow. I loaded my gun and examined the place which was dusty and saw the track from which I am still further convinced that it was of the tiger kind.[6] . . .

It now seemed to me that all the beasts of the neighbourhood had made a league to distroy me, or that some fortune was disposed to amuse herself at my expence, for I had not proceded more than three hundred yards from the burrow of this tyger cat, before three bull buffaloes which wer feeding with a large herd about half a mile from me on my left, separated from the herd and ran full speed towards me. I thought at least to give them some amusement and altered my direction to meet them. When they arrived within a hundred yards they made a halt, took a good view of me and retreated with precipitation. I then continued my rout homewards passed the buffaloe which I had killed, but did not think it prudent to remain all night at this place which really from the succession of curious adventures wore the impression on my mind of enchantment; at sometimes for a moment I thought it might be a dream, but the prickley pears which pierced my feet very severely once in a while, particularly after it grew dark, convinced me that I was really awake, and that it was necessary to make the best of my way to camp.

[Lewis] June 15, 1805

When I awoke from my sleep today I found a large rattlesnake coiled on the leaning trunk of a tree under the shade of which I had been lying at the distance of about ten feet from him. I killed the snake and found that he had 176 scuta on the abdomen and 17 half formed scuta on the tale.

The following morning Lewis left his camp at the base of the falls and rejoined Clark, who was still making his way up the "south fork," which they now knew to be the main branch of the Missouri.

[Lewis] June 16, 1805

I reached the camp; found the Indian woman extreemly ill and much reduced by her indisposition. This gave me some concern as well for the poor object herself, then with a young child in her arms, as from the consideration of her being our only dependence for a friendly negociation with the Snake Indians on whom we depend for horses to assist us in our portage from the Missouri to the columbia river. . . . I found that two dozes of barks and opium which I had given her since my arrival had produced an alteration in her pulse for the better; they were now much fuller and more regular. I caused her to drink the mineral water altogether. W[h]en I first came down I found that her pulse were scarcely perceptible, very quick frequently irregular and attended with strong nervous symptoms, that of the twitching of the fingers and leaders of the arm; now the pulse had become regular much fuller and a gentle perspiration had taken place. The nervous symptoms have also in a great measure abated, and she feels herself much freer from pain. She complains principally of the lower region of the abdomen. I therefore continued the cataplasms of barks and laudnumn which had been previously used by my friend Capt. Clark. I beleive her disorder originated principally from an obstruction of the mensis in consequence of taking could.

[Clark] June 16, 1805

The Indian woman verry bad, & will take no medisin what ever, untill her husband finding her out of her sences, easyly provailed on her to take medison. If she dies it will be the fault of her husband as I am now convinced.

[Lewis] June 19, 1805

The Indian woman was much better this morning. She walked out and gathered a considerable quantity of the white apples of which she eat so heartily in their raw state, together with a considerable quantity of dryed fish without my knowledge that she complained very much and her fever again returned. I rebuked Sharbono severely for suffering her to indulge herself with such food he being privy to it and having been previously told what she must only eat. I now gave her broken dozes of diluted nitre untill it produced perspiration and at 10 p.m. 30 drops of laudnum which gave her a tolerable nights rest.

[Lewis] June 20, 1805

The mountains to the N.W. and west of us are still entirely covered are white and glitter with the reflection of the sun. I do not believe that the clouds that pervale at this season of the year reach the summits of those lofty mountains; and if they do the probability is that they deposit snow only for there has been no proceptable diminution of the snow which they contain since we first saw them. I have thought it probable that these mountains might have derived their appellation of Shining Mountains, from their glittering appearance when the sun shines in certain directions on the snow which cover them.

Dureing the time of my being on the plains and above the falls I as also all my party repeatedly heard a nois which proceeded from a direction a little to the N. of west, a loud [noise] and resembling precisely the discharge of a piece of ordinance of 6 pounds at the distance of 5 or six miles. I was informed of it several times by the men J. Fields particularly before I paid any attention to it, thinking it was thunder most probably which they had mistaken. At length walking in the plains yesterday near the most extreem S.E. bend of the river above the falls I heard this nois very distinctly, it was perfectly calm clear and not a cloud to be seen, I halted and listened attentively about two hour[s] dureing which time I heard two other discharges, and took the direction of the sound with my pocket compass which was as nearly West from me as I could estimate from the sound. I have no doubt but if I had leasure I could find from whence it issued . . . it is heard also at different times of the day and night. I am at a great loss to account for this phenomenon. I well recollect hereing the Minitarees say that those Rocky Mountains make a great noise, but they could not tell me the cause, neither could they inform me of any remarkable substance or situation in these mountains which would autherise a conjecture of a probable cause of this noise.

At the Mandan Villages, Lewis and Clark had been told that they would have to make only a short portage around the Great Falls of the Missouri. Instead, on June 22 they began an arduous overland journey, carrying and pushing several tons of equipment, that eventually took almost a full month.

[Lewis] June 23, 1805

This evening the men repaired their mockersons, and put on double souls to protect their feet from the prickley pears. During the late rains the buffaloe have troden up the praire very much which having now become dry the sharp points of earth as hard as frozen ground standup in such abundance that there is no avoiding them. This is particularly severe on the feet of the men who have not only their own weight to bear in treading on those hacklelike points but have also the addition of the burthen which they draw and which in fact is as much as they can possibly move with. They are obliged to halt and rest frequently for a few minutes. At every halt these poor fellow tumble down and are so much fortiegued that many of them are asleep in an instant. In short, their fatiegues are incredible; some are limping from the soreness of their feet, others faint and unable to stand for a few minutes, with heat and fatigue, yet no one complains. All go with cheerfullness.

[Lewis] June 27, 1805

A bear came within thirty yards of our camp last night and eat up about thirty weight of buffaloe suit which was hanging on a pole. My dog seems to be in a constant state of alarm with these bear and keeps barking all night . . .

[Lewis] June 29, 1805

On his arrival at the falls he [Clark] perceived a very black cloud rising in the west which threatened immediate rain; he

looked about for a shelter but could fine none without being in
great danger of being blown into the river should the wind prove
as violent as it sometimes is on those occasions in these plains; at
length about a ¼ of a mile above the falls he discovered a deep
rivene where there were some shelving rocks under which he took
shelter near the river with Sharbono and the Indian woman, laying their guns compass &c. under a shelving rock on the upper side
of the rivene where they were perfectly secure from the rain.

The first shower was moderate accompanyed by a violent rain
the effects of which they did but little feel. Soon after a most violent torrent of rain decended accompanyed with hall. The rain
appeared to decend in a body and instantly collected in the rivene
and came down in a roling torrent with irrisistable force driving
rocks mud and everything before it which opposed it's passage.
Capt. C. fortunately discovered it a moment before it reached
them and seizing his gun and shot pouch with his left hand with
the right he assisted himself up the steep bluff shoving occasionally
the Indian woman before him who had her child in her arms.
Sharbono had the woman by the hand indeavouring to pull her up
the hill but was so much frightned that he remained frequently
motionless and but for Capt. C. both himself and his woman and
child must have perished. So suddon was the rise of the water that
before Capt. C. could reach his gun and begin to ascend the bank it
was up to his waist and wet his watch, and he could scarcely ascent
faster than it arrose till it had obtained the debth of 15 with a current tremendious to behold. One moment longer & it would have
swept them into the river just above the great cataract of 87 feet
where they must have inevitably perished.

Sharbono lost his gun, shot pouch, horn, tomahawk, and my
wiping rod. Cap' Clark his umbrella and compass or circurnfer-
enter. They fortunately arrived on the plain safe, where they found
the black man, York, in surch of them. York had separated from

them a little while before the storm, in pursuit of some buffaloe and had not seen them enter the rivene. When this gust came on he returned in surch of them & not being able to find them for some time was much allarmed. The bier in which the woman carrys her child and all it's cloaths wer swept away as they lay at her feet she having time only to grasp her child; the infant was therefore very cold and the woman also who had just recovered from a severe indisposition was also wet and cold.

Capt. C. therefore relinquished his intended rout and returned to the camp at willow run in order also to obtain dry cloathes for himself and directed them to follow him. On Capt. Clark's arrival at camp he found that the party dispatched for the baggage had returned in great confusion and consternation leaving their loads in the plains. The men who were all nearly naked and [no] covering on the head were sorely mawled with the hail which was so large and driven with such force by the wind that it nocked many of them down and one particularly as many as three times most of them were bleeding freely and complained of being much bruised. Capt. C. gave the party a dram to console them in some measure for their general defeat.

[Lewis] July 4, 1805

Not having seen the Snake Indians or knowing in fact whether to calculate on their friendship or hostility or friendship we have conceived our party sufficiently small and therefore have concluded not to dispatch a canoe with a part of our men to St. Louis as we had intended early in the spring. We fear also that such a measure might possibly discourage those who would in such case remain, and might possibly hazzard the fate of the expedition. We have never once hinted to any one of the party that we had such a scheme in contemplation, and all appear perfectly to have made up their minds to suceed in the expedition or purish in the attempt.

This evening, we gave the men a drink of sperits, it being the last of our stock, and some of them appeared a little sensible of it's effects. The fiddle was plyed, and they danced very merrily untill 9 in the evening when a heavy shower of rain put an end to that part of the amusement tho' they continued their mirth with songs and festive jokes and were extreemly merry untill late at night.

We had a very comfortable dinner, of bacon, beans, suit dumplings & buffaloe beaf &c. In short we had no just cause to covet the sumptuous feasts of our countrymen on this day.

[Lewis] July 19, 1805

This evening we entered much the most remarkable clifts that we have yet seen. These clifts rise from the waters edge on either side perpendicularly to the hight of (about) 1200 feet. Every object here wears a dark and gloomy aspect. The towering and projecting rocks in many places seem ready to tumble on us. This rock is a black grannite below and appears to be of a much lighter colour above and from the fragments I take it to be flint of a yellowish brown and light creem coloured yellow. From the singular appearance of this place I called it *the gates of the rocky mounatains.*

[Lewis] July 22, 1805

The Indian woman recognizes the country and assures us that this is the river on which her relations live, and that the three forks are at no great distance. This peice of information has cheered the sperits of the party who now begin to console themselves with the anticipation of shortly seeing the head of the Missouri, yet unknown to the civilized world.

[Lewis] July 24, 1805

Our trio of pests still invade and obstruct us on all occasions. These are the musquetoes, eye knats and prickley pears, equal to any three curses that ever poor Egypt laiboured under, except the Mahometant yoke.

The men complain of being much fortiegued. Their labour is excessively great. I occasionly encourage them by assisting in the labour of navigating the canoes, and have learned to push a tolerable good pole.

[Lewis] July 26, 1805

The high lands are thin meagre soil covered with dry low sedge and a species of grass also dry the seeds of which are armed with a long twisted hard beard at the upper extremity while the lower point is a sharp subulate, firmpoint beset at it's base with little stiff bristles standing with their points in a contrary direction to the subulate point to which they answer as a barb and serve also to pres it forward when onece entered a small distance. These barbed seed penetrate our mockersons and leather legings and give us great pain untill they are removed. My poor dog suffers with them excessively, he is constantly binting and scratching himself as if in a rack of pain.

[Lewis] July 27, 1805

We arrived at 9 a.m. at the junction of the S.E. fork of the Missouri and the country opens suddonly to extensive and beautifull plains and meadows which appear to be surrounded in every direction with distant and lofty mountains. Supposing this to be the three forks of the Missouri I halted the party for breakfast and . . . ascended the point of a high limestone clift from whence I commanded a most perfect view of the neighbouring country.

Capt. Clark arrived very sick with a high fever on him and much fatiegued and exhausted. He informed me that he was very sick last night had a high fever and frequent chills & constant pains in all his mustles. . . . Capt. C. thought himself somewhat bilious and had not had a passage for several days. I prevailed on him to take a doze of Rushes pills, which I have always found sovereign in such cases and to bath his feet in warm water and rest himself.

We begin to feel considerable anxiety with rispect to the Snake Indians. If we do not find them or some other nation who have horses I fear the successfull issue of our voyage will be very doubtfull or at all events much more difficult in it's accomplishment. We are now several hundred miles within the bosom of this wild and mountanous country, where game may rationally be expected shortly to become scarce and subsistence precarious without any information with rispect to the country not knowing how far these mountains continue, or wher to direct our course to pass them to advantage or intersept a navigable branch of the Columbia, or even were we on such an one the probability is that we should not find any timber within these mountains large enough for canoes if we judge from the portion of them through which we have passed.

However I still hope for the best, and intend taking a tramp myself in a few days to find these yellow gentlemen if possible. My two principal consolations are that from our present position it is impossible that the S.W. fork can head with the waters of any other river but the Columbia, and that if any Indians can subsist in the form of a nation in these mountains with the means they have of acquiring food we can also subsist.

[Lewis] July 28, 1805

My friend Capt. Clark was very sick all last night but feels himself somewhat better this morning since his medicine has opperated. . . . Both Capt. C. and myself corrisponded in opinon with rispect to the impropriety of calling either of these streams the Missouri and accordingly agreed to name them after the President of the United States and the Secretaries of the Treasury and state having previously named one river in honour of the Secretaries of

War and Navy. In pursuance of this resolution we called the S.W. fork, that which we meant to ascend, Jefferson's River in honor of that illustrious personage Thomas Jefferson. [*the author of our enterprize*.] The middle fork we called Madison's River in honor of James Madison, and the S.E. fork we called Gallitin's River in honor of Albert Gallitin.

Our present camp is precisely on the spot that the Snake Indians were encamped at the time the Minnetares of the Knif'e R. first came in sight of them five years since. From hence they retreated about three miles up Jeffersons river and concealed themselves in the woods. The Minnetares pursued, attacked them, killed 4 men 4 women a number of boys, and made prisoners of all the females and four boys. *Sah-cah-gar-we-ah* our Indian woman was one of the female prisoners taken at that time; tho' I cannot discover that she shews any immotion of sorrow in recollecting this event, or of joy in being again restored to her native country; if she has enough to eat and a few trinkets to wear I beleive she would be perfectly content anywhere.

[Lewis] August 3, 1805

Capt. Clark . . . saw a track which he supposed to be that of an Indian from the circumstance of the large toes turning inward. He pursued the track and found that the person had ascended a point of the hill from which his camp of the last evening was visible. This circumstance also confirmed the beleif of it's being an Indian who had thus discovered them and ran off. . . . This morning they passed a small creek at the entrance of which Reubin Fields killed a large panther [which] measured seven and ½ feet from the nose to the extremity of the tail.

As he often did, Lewis walked upstream on the shore with several men, leaving Clark, the more accomplished waterman, to bring the canoes up

the Jefferson. At the site of the present-day Twin Bridges, Montana, the
stream forked twice. Lewis named the two branches the Philanthrophy
(today's Ruby) and the Wisdom (today's Big Hole). The middle branch is
today's Beaverhead. Here he pondered which river to follow.

[Lewis] August 4, 1805

The middle fork is gentle and possesses about ²/₃rds. as much
water as this rapid stream. It's course so far as I can observe is
about S.W. and it appears to be navigable; its water is much
warmer than that of the rappid fork and somewhat turbid, from
which I concluded that it has it's source as a greater distance in the
mountains and passed through an opener country than the other.
Under this impression I wrote a note to Capt. Clark recommend-
ing his taking the middle fork. . . . This note I left on a pole at the
forks of the river.

[Clark] August 4, 1805

I could not walk on shore to day as my ankle was sore from a
turner on that part. The method we are compelled to take to get on is
fatigueing & laborious in the extreen. Haul the canoes over the rapids,
which suckceed each other every two or three hundred yards and
between the water rapid oblige to tow & walke on stones the whole
day except when we have poleing. Men wet all day sore feet &c. &c.

[Lewis] August 5, 1805

This morning Capt. Clark set out at sunrise . . . the river today
they found straighter and more rapid even than yesterday . . . they
therefore proceeded but slowly and with great pain as the men had
become very languid from working in the water and many of their
feet swolen and so painfull that they could scarcely walk. At 4 P.M.
they arrived at the confluence the two rivers where I had left the

note. This note had unfortunately been placed on a green pole which the beaver had cut and carried off together with the note. The possibility of such an occurrence never once occurred to me when I placed it on the green pole.

[Lewis] August 6, 1805

Shannon had been dispatched up the rapid fork this morning to hunt, before he [Clark] met with Drewyer or learnt of his mistake in the rivers. When he returned he sent Drewyer in surch of [Shannon], but he rejoined us this evening and could find nothing of him. We had the trumpet sounded and fired several guns but he did not join us this evening. I am fearful he is lost again. This is the same man who was seperated from us 15 days as we came up the Missouri and subsisted 9 days of that time on grapes only.

[Lewis] August 8, 1805

The tumor on Capt. Clarks ankle has discharged a considerable quantity of matter but is still much swolen and inflamed and gives him considerable pain. The Indian woman recognized the point of a high plain to our right which she informed us was not very distant from the summer retreat of her nation on a river beyond the mountains which runs to the west. This hill she says her nation calls the beaver's head from a conceived resemblance of it's figure to the head of that animal.

She assures us that we shall either find her people on this river or on the river immediately west of it's source; which from it's present size cannot be very distant. As it is now all important with us to meet with those people as soon as possible I determined to proceed tomorrow with a small party to the source of the principal stream of this river and pass the mountains to the Columbia; and down that river untill I found the Indians; in short it is my resolusion to find them or some others, who have horses if it should cause me a trip of one month.

At the forks of the Beaverhead, just south of the present Dillon, Montana, Lewis turned west on Horse Prairie Creek.

[Lewis] August 11, 1805

I therefore resolved to proceed on the creek about 10 miles West in hopes that I should again find the Indian road. . . . I now sent Drewyer to keep near the creek to my right and Shields to my left, with orders to surch for the road which if they found they were to notify me by placing a hat in the muzzle of their gun. I kept McNeal with me. After having marched in this order for about five miles I discovered an Indian on horse back about two miles distant coming down the plain towards us. With my glass I discovered from his dress that he was of a different nation from any that we had yet seen, and was satisfyed of his being a Sosone; his arms were a bow and quiver of arrows, and was mounted on an eligant horse without a saddle, and a small string which was attatched to the under jaw of the horse which answered as a bridle.

I was overjoyed at the sight of this stranger and had no doubt of obtaining a friendly introduction to his nation provided I could get near enough to him to convince him of our being white men. I therefore proceeded towards him at my usual pace. When I had arrived within about a mile he made a halt which I did also and unloosing my blanket from my pack, I made him the signal of friendship known to the Indians of the Rocky mountains and those of the Missouri, which is by holding the mantle or robe in your hands at two corners and then throwing [it] up in the air higher than the head bringing it to the earth as in the act of spreading it, thus repeating three times. This signal of the robe has arrisen from a custom among all those nations of spreading a robe or skin for ther gests to set on when they are visited. This signal had not the desired effect, he still kept his position and seemed to view Drewyer and Shields who were now comiming in sight on either hand with an air of suspicion.

I would willingly have made them halt but they were too far distant to hear me and I feared to make any signal to them least it should increase the suspicion in the mind of the Indian of our having some unfriendly design upon him. I therefore haistened to take out of my sack some beads a looking glas and a few trinkets which I had brought with me for this purpose and leaving my gun and pouch with McNeal advanced unarmed towards him. He remained in the same stedfast poisture untill I arrived in about 200 paces of him when he turn[ed] his ho[r]se about and began to move off slowly from me; I now called to him in a loud a voice as I could command repearing the word *tab-ba-bone*, which in their language signifyes *white-man*. But looking over his sholder he still kept his eye on Drewyer and Sheilds who wer still advancing neither of them having segacity enough to recollet the impropriety of advancing when they saw me thus in parley with the Indian. I now made a signal to these men to halt. Drewyer obeyed but Shields who afterwards told me that he did not observe the signal still kept on. The Indian halted again and turned his horse about as if to wait for me, and I believe he would have remained untill I came up with him had it not been for Shields who still pressed forward.

When I arrived within about 150 paces I again repepeated the word *tab-ba-bone* and held my the trinkits in my hands and striped up my shirt sleve to give him an opportunity of seeing the colour of my skin and advanced leasurely towards him. But he did not remain untill I got nearer than about 100 paces when he suddonly turned his horse about, give him the whip, leaped the creek and disapeared in the willow brush in an instant and with him vanished all my hopes of obtaining horses for the preasent.

I now felt quite as much mortification and disappointment as I had pleasure and expectation at the first sight of this Indian. I felt soarly chargrined at the conduct of the men particularly Sheilds to whom I principally attributed this failure in obtaining an introduction to the natives. I now called the men to me and could not forbare abraiding them a little for their want of attention and imprudence on this occasion. They had neglected to bring my spye-glass which in haist I had droped in the plain with the blanket where I made the signal before mentioned. I sent Drewyer and Shields back to surche it, they soon found it and rejoined me.

We pursued the track of the horse but as the rain had raised the grass which he had trodden down it was with difficulty that we could follow it . . . we passed several places where the Indians appeared to have been diging roots today and saw the fresh tracks of 8 or ten horses but they had been wandering about in such a confused manner that we not only lost the track of the horse which we had been pursuing but could make nothing of them. . . . After meeting with the Indian today I fixed a small flag of the U.S. to a pole which I made McNeal carry and planted in the ground where we halted or encamped.

[Lewis] August 12, 1805

This morning I sent Drewyer out as soon as it was light to try and discover what rout the Indians had taken. He followed the track of the horse we had pursued yesterday to the mountain wher it had ascended, and returned to me in about an hour and a half . . . the main stream now after discarding two stream[s] on the left in this valley turns abruptly to the west through a narrow bottom between the mountains. The road was still plain. I therefore did not dispair of shortly finding a passage over the mountains and of taisting the waters of the great Columbia this evening. . . .

At the distance of 4 miles further the road took us to the most distant fountain of the waters of the Mighty Missouri in surch of which we have spent so many toilsome days and wristless nights. Thus far I had accomplished one of those great objects on which my mind has been unalterably fixed for many years. Judge then of the pleasure I felt in allaying my thirst with this pure and ice-cold water which issues from the base of a low mountain or hill of a gentle ascent for ½ a mile. The mountains are high on either hand leave this gap at the head of this rivulet through which the road passes. Here I halted a few minutes and rested myself. Two miles below McNeal had exultingly stood with a foot on each side of this little rivulet and thanked his god that he had lived to bestride the mighty & heretofore deemed endless Missouri.

After refreshing ourselves we proceeded on to the top of the dividing ridge[7] from which I discovered immence ranges of high mountains still to the west of us with their tops partially covered with snow. I now decended the mountain about 3/4 of a mile which I found much steeper than on the opposite side, to a handsome bold runing creek of cold clear water. here I first tasted the water of the great Columbia River.[8]

[Lewis] August 13, 1805

We set out very early on the Indian road which still led us through an open broken country in a westerly direction . . . at the distance of about a mile we saw two women, a man and some dogs on an eminence immediately before us. They appeared to view us with attention and two of them after a few minutes set down as if to wait our arrival we continued our usual pace towards them. When we had arrived within half a mile of them I directed the party to halt and leaving my pack and rifle I took the flag which I unfurled and advanced singly towards them. The women soon disappeared behind the hill. The man continued untill I arrived within a hundred yards of him and then likewise absconded tho' I frequently repeated the word *tab-ba-bone* sufficiently loud for him to have heard it. I now haistened to the top of the hill where they had stood but could see nothing of them. The dogs were less shye than their masters they came about me pretty close I therefore thought of tying a handkerchief about one of their necks with some beads and other trinkets and then let them loose to surch their fugitive owners thinking by this means to convince them of our pacific disposition towards them but the dogs would not suffer me to take hold of them; they also soon disappeared.

We had not continued our rout more than a mile when we were so fortunate as to meet with three female savages. The short and steep ravines which we passed concealed us from each other untill we arrived within 30 paces. A young woman immediately took to flight. An elderly woman and a girl of about 12 years old remained. I instantly laid by my gun and advanced towards them. They appeared much allarmed but saw that we were to[o] near for them to escape by flight they therefore seated themselves on the ground, holding down their heads as if reconciled to die which they expected no doubt would be their fate. I took the elderly woman by the hand and raised her up repeated the word *tab-ba-bone* and stripped up my shirt sleve to shew her my skin; to prove to her the truth of the ascertion that I was a white man for my face and hands which have been constantly exposed to the sun were quite as dark as their own.

They appeared instantly reconciled, and the men coming up I gave these women some beads a few mockerson awls some pewter looking-glasses and a little paint. I directed Drewyer to request the old woman to recall the young woman who had run off to some distance by this time fearing she might allarm the camp before we approached and might so exasperate the natives that they would perhaps attack us without enquiring who we were. The old woman did as she was requested and the fugitive soon returned almost out of breath. I bestoed an equivolent portion of trinket on her with the others. I now painted their tawny cheeks with some vermillion which with this nation is emblematic of peace. After they had become composed I enformed them by signs that I wished them to conduct us to their camp that we wer anxious to become acquainted with the chiefs and warriors of their nation. They readily obeyed and we set out, still pursuing the road down the river.

We had marched about 2 miles when we met a party of about 60 warriors mounted on excellent horses who came in nearly full speed. When they arrived I advanced towards them with the flag leaving my gun with the party about 50 paces behind me. The chief and two others who were a little in advance of the main body spoke to the women, and they informed them who we were and exultingly shewed the presents which had been given them. These men then advanced and embraced me very affectionately in their way which is by puting their left arm over your wright sholder clasping your back, while they apply their left cheek to yours and frequently vociferate the word *a'h-hi-e, a'h-hi-e,* that is, I am much pleased, I am much rejoiced. Bothe parties now advanced and we wer all carresed and besmeared with their grease and paint till I was heartily tired of the national hug.

I now had the pipe lit and gave them smoke. They seated themselves in a circle around us and pulled off their mockersons before they would receive or smoke the pipe. This is a custom among them as I afterwards learned indicative of a sacred obligation of sincerity in their profession of friendship given by the act of receiving and smoking the pipe of a stranger. Or which is as much as to say that they wish they may always go bearfoot if they are not sincere; a pretty heavy penalty if they are to march through the plains of their country.

After smoking a few pipes with them I distributed some trifles among them, with which they seemed much pleased particularly with the blue beads and vermillion.

I now informed the chief that the object of our visit was a friendly one, that after we should reach his camp I would undertake to explain to him fiilly those objects, who we wer, from whence we had come and w[h]ither we were going; that in the mean time I did not care how soon we were in motion, as the sun was very warm and no water at hand. They now put on their mockersons, and the principal chief Ca-me-a'h-wait made a short speach to the warriors. I gave him the flag which I informed him was an emblem of peace among whitemen and now that it had been received by him it was to be respected as the bond of union between us. I desired him to march on, which [he] did and we followed him; the dragoons moved on squadron in our rear. After we had marched about a mile in this order he halted them and gave a second harang; after which six or eight of the young men road forward to their encampment and no further regularity was observed in the order of march. I afterwards understood that the Indians we had first seen this morning had returned and allarmed the camp; these men had come out armed for action expecting to meet with their enimies the Minnetares of Fort de Prarie whome they call Pah'-kees.

They introduced us to a lodge made of willow brush and an old leather lodge which had been prepared for our reception by the young men which the chief had dispatched for that purpose. Here we were seated on green boughs and the skins of antelopes. One of the warriors then pulled up the grass in the center of the lodge forming a small circle of about 2 feet in diameter the chief next produced his pipe and native tobacco and began a long cerimony of the pipe when we were requested to take off our mockersons, the chief having previously taken off his as well as all the warriors present. This we complyed with.

The chief then lit his pipe at the fire kindled in this little magic circle, and standing on the oposite side of the circle uttered a speach of several minutes in length at the conclusion of which he pointed the stem to the four cardinal points of the heavens first begining at the east and ending with the north. He now presented the pipe to me as if desirous that I should smoke, but when I reached my hand to receive it, he drew it back and repeated the same ceremony three times, after which he pointed the stem first to the heavens then to the center of the magic circle smoked himself with three whifs and held the pipe untill I took as many as I thought proper. He then held it to each of the white persons and then gave it to be consumed by his warriors. . . . I now explained to them the objects of our journey &c. All the women and children of the camp were shortly collected about the lodge to indulge themselves with looking at us, we being the first white persons they had ever seen. After the cerimony of the pipe was over I distributed the remainder of the small articles I had brought with me among the women and children.

By this time it was late in the evening and we had not taisted any food since the evening before. The chief informed us that they had nothing but berries to eat and gave us some cakes of service berries and choke cherries which had been dryed in the sun. Of these I made a hearty meal, and then walked to the river, which I found about 40 yards wide very rapid clear and about 3 feet deep. The banks low and abrupt as those of the upper part of the Missouri, and the bed formed of loose stones and gravel.

Cameahwait informed me that this stream discharged itself into another doubly as large at the distance of half a days march which came from the S.W. but he added on further enquiry that there was but little more timber below the junction of those rivers than I saw here, and that the river was confined between inacessable mountains, was very rapid and rocky insomuch that it was impossible for us to pass either by land or water down this river to the great lake where the white men lived as he had been informed.

This was unwelcome information but I still hoped that this account had been exagerated with a view to detain us among them. As to timber I could discover not any that would answer the purpose of constructing canoes or in short more than was bearly necessary for fuel consisting of the narrow leafed cottonwood and willow, also the red willow choke cherry service berry and a few currant bushes such as were common on the Missouri. These people had been attacked by the Minetares of Fort de Prarie this spring and about 20 of them killed and taken prisoners. On this occasion they lost a great part of their horses and all their lodges except that which they had erected for our accomodation; they were now living in lodges of a conic figure made of willow brush. I still observe a great number of horses feeding in every direction around their camp and therefore entertain but little doubt but we shall be enable[d] to furnish ourselves with an adiquate number to transport our stores even if we are compelled to travel by land over these mountains.

On my return to my lodge an Indian called me in to his bower and gave me a small morsel of the flesh of an antelope boiled, and a peice of a fresh salmon roasted; both which I eat with a very good relish. This was the first salmon I had seen and perfectly convinced me that we were on the waters of the Pacific Ocean.

This evening the Indians entertained us with their dancing nearly all night. At 12 O'Ck I grew sleepy and retired to rest leaving the men to amuse themselves with the Indians. I observe no essential difference between the music and manner of dancing among this nation and those of the Missouri. I was several times awoke in the course of the night by their yells but was too much fortiegued to be deprived of a tolerable sound night's repose.

[Lewis] August 14, 1805

In order to give Capt. Clark time to reach the forks of Jefferson's River I concluded to spend this day at the Shoshone Camp and obtain what information I could with rispect to the country. As we had nothing but a little flour and parched meal to eat except the berries with which the Indians furnished us I directed Drewyer and Shields to hunt a few hours and try to kill something. The Indians furnished them with horses and most of their young men also turned out to hunt. The game which they principally hunt is the antelope which they pursue on horseback and shoot with their arrows. This animal is so extreemly fleet and dureable that a single horse has no possible chance to overtake them or run them down.

The Indians are therefore obliged to have recorce to stratagem when they discover a herd of the antelope they seperate and scatter themselves to the distance of five or six miles in different directions arround them generally scelecting some comanding eminence for a stand; some one or two now pursue the herd at full speed over the hills vallies gullies and the sides of precipices that are tremendious to view. Thus after runing them from five to six or seven miles the fresh horses that were in waiting head them and drive them back persuing them as far or perhaps further quite to the other extreem of the hunters who now in turn pursue on their fresh horses thus worrying the poor animal down and finally killing them with their arrows. Forty or fifty hunters will be engaged for haf a day in this manner and perhaps not kill more than two or three antelopes. I was very much entertained with a view of this Indian chase; it was after a herd of about 10 antelope and about 20 hunters. It lasted about 2 hours and considerable part of the chase in view from my tent. About 1. a.m. the hunters returned had not killed a single antelope, and their horses foaming with sweat. My hunters returned soon after and had been equally unsuccessfull. I now directed McNeal to make me a little paist with the flour and added some berries to it which I found very pallatable.

The means I had of communicating with these people was by way of Drewyer who understood perfectly the common language of gesticulation or signs which seems to be universally understood by all the Nations we have yet seen. It is true that this language is imperfect and liable to error but is much less so than would be expected. The strong parts of the ideas are seldom mistaken. I now told Cameahwait that I wished him to speak to his people and engage them to go with me tomorrow to the forks of Jeffersons River where our baggage was by this time arrived with another chief and a large party of white men who would wait my return at that place; that I wish them to take with them about 30 spare horses to transport our baggage to this place where we would then remain sometime among them and trade with them for horses, and finally concert our future plans for geting on to the ocean and of the traid which would be extended to them after our return to our homes.

He complyed with my request and made a lengthey harrangue to his village. He returned in about an hour and a half and informed me that they would be ready to accompany me in the morning. I promised to reward them for their trouble. Drewyer who had had a good view of their horses estimated them at 400. Most of them are fine horses. Indeed many of them would make a figure on the south side of James River or the land of fine horses. I saw several with Spanish brands on them, and some mules which they informed me that they had also obtained from the Spaniards. I also saw a bridle bit of Spanish manufactary, and sundry other articles which I have no doubt were obtained from the same source. Notwithstanding the extreem poverty of those poor people they are very merry. They danced again this evening untill midnight. Each warrior keeps one or more horses tyed by a cord to a stake near his lodge both day and night and are always prepared for action at a moments warning. They fight on horseback altogether.

This evening Charbono struck his Indian woman for which Capt. C. gave him a severe repremand.

This morning I arrose very early and as hungary as a wolf.

I had eat nothing yesterday except one scant meal of the flour and berries except the dryed cakes of berries which did not appear to satisfy my appetite as they appeared to do those of my Indian friends. I found on enquiry of McNeal that we had only about two pounds of flour remaining. This I directed him to divide into two equal parts and to cook the one half this morning in a kind of pudding with the burries as he had done yesterday and reserve the ballance for the evening. On this new fashoned pudding four of us breakfasted, giving a pretty good allowance also to the chief who declared it the best thing he had taisted for a long time. He took a little of the flour in his hand, taisted and examined [it] very scrutinously and asked me if we made it of roots. I explained to him the manner in which it grew.

I hurried the departure of the Indians. The chief addressed them several times before they would move they seemed very reluctant to accompany me. I at length asked the reason and he told me that some foolish persons among them had suggested the idea that we were in league with the Pahkees and had come on in order to decoy them into an ambuscade where their enimies were waiting to receive them. But that for his part he did not believe it. I readily perceived that our situation was not enterely free from danger as the transicion from suspicion to the confermation of the fact would not be very difficult in the minds of these ignorant people who have been accustomed from their infancy to view every stranger as an eminy.

I told Cameahwait that I was sorry to find that they had put so little confidence in us, that I knew they were not acquainted with whitemen and therefore could forgive them. That among whitemen it was considered disgracefull to lye or entrap an enimy by falsehood. I told him if they continued to think thus meanly of us that they might rely on it that no whitemen would ever come to trade with them or bring them arms and ammunition and that if the bulk of his nation still entertained this opinion I still hoped that there were some among them that were not affraid to die, that were men and would go with me and convince themselves of the truth of what I had asscerted. That there was a party of whitemen waiting my return either at the forks of Jefferson's River or a little below coming on to that place in canoes loaded with provisions and merchandise.

He told me for his own part he was determined to go, that he was not affraid to die. I soon found that I had touched him on the right string; to doubt the bravery of a savage is at once to put him on his metal. He now mounted his horse and haranged his village a third time; the perport of which as he afterwards told me was to inform them that he would go with us and convince himself of the truth or falsity of what we had told him. If he was sertain he should be killed, that he hoped there were some of them who heard him were not affraid to die with him and if there was to let him see them mount their horses and prepare to set out. Shortly after this harange he was joined by six or eight only and with these I smoked a pipe and directed the men to put on their packs being determined to set out with them while I had them in the humour. At half after 12 we set out, several of the old women were crying and imploring the great sperit to protect their warriors as if they were going to inevitable destruction.

We had not proceeded far before our part was augmented by ten or twelve more, and before we reached the creek which we had passed in the morning of the 13th it appeared to me that we had all the men of the village and a number of women with us. This may serve in some manner to illustrate the capricious disposition of those people, who never act but from the impulse of the moment. They were now very cheerfall and gay and two hours ago they looked as sirly as so many imps of satturn.

When we arrived at the spring on the side of the mountain where we had encamped on the 12th the chief insisted on halting to let the horses graize with which I complyed and gave the Indian smoke. They are excessively fond of the pipe; but have it not much in their power to indulge themselves with even their native tobacco as they do not cultivate it themselves. After remaining about an hour we again set out, and by engaging to make compensation to four of them for their trouble obtained the previlege of riding with an indian myself and a similar situation for each of my party. I soon found it more tiresome riding without stirrups than walking and of course chose the latter making the Indian carry my pack. About sunset we reached the upper part of the level valley of the cove which [we] now called Shoshone Cove.

[Lewis] August 16, 1805

I sent Drewyer and Shields before this morning in order to kill some meat as neither the Indians nor ourselves had any thing to eat. I informed the c[h]eif of my view in this measure, and requested that he would keep his young men with us lest by their hooping and noise they should allarm the game and we should get nothing to eat. But so strongly were there suspicions exited by this measure that two parties of discovery immediately set out one on e[a]ch side of the valley to watch the hunters as I beleive to see whether they had not been sent to give information of their approach to an enemy that they still preswaided themselves were lying in wait for them. I saw that any further effort to prevent their going would only add strength to their suspicions and therefore said no more.

After the hunters had been gone about an hour we set out. We had just passed through the narrows when we saw one of the spies comeing up the level plain under whip. The chief pawsed a little and seemed somewhat concerned. I felt a good deel so myself and began to suspect that by some unfortunate accedent that perhaps some of there enimies had straggled hither at this unlucky moment; but we were all agreeably disappointed on the arrival of the young man to learn that he had come to inform us that one of the white men had killed a deer. In an instant they all gave their horses the whip and I was taken nearly a mile before I could learn what were the tidings. As I was without stirrups and an Indian behind me the jostling was disagreeable I therefore reigned up my horse and forbid the Indian to whip him who had given him the lash at every jump for a mile fearing he should loose a part of the feast. The fellow was so uneasy that he left me the horse dismounted and ran on foot at full speed I am confident a mile.

When they arrived where the deer was which was in view of me they dismounted and ran in tumbling over each other like a parcel of famished dogs each seizing and tearing away a part of the intestens which had been previously thrown out by Drewyer who killed it.

The seen was such when I arrived that had I not have had a pretty keen appetite myself I am confident I should not have taisted any part of the venison shortly. Each one had a peice of some description and all eating most ravenously. Some were eating the kidnies the melt and liver and the blood runing from the corners of their mouths. Others were in a similar situation with the paunch and guts but the exuding substance in this case from their lips was of a different description. One of the last who attracted my attention particularly had been fortunate in his allotment or reather active in the division. He had provided himself with about nine feet of the small guts one end of which he was chewing on while with his hands he was squezzing the contents out at the other.

I really did not untill now think that human nature ever presented itself in a shape so nearly allyed to the brute creation. I viewed

these poor starved divils with pity and compassion. I directed
McNeal to skin the deer and reserved a quarter. The ballance I gave
the chief to be divided among his people; they devoured the whole of
it nearly without cooking. I now boar obliquely to the left in order to
interscept the creek where there was some brush to make a fire, and
arrived at this stream where Drewyer had killed a second deer. Here
nearly the same seene was enacted. A fire being kindled we cooked
and eat and gave the ballance of the two deer to the Indians who eat
the whole of them even to the soft parts of the hoofs. Drewyer joined
us at breakfast with a third deer. Of this I reserved a quarter and gave
the ballance to the Indians. They all appeared now to have filled
themselves and were in a good humour.

This morning early soon after the hunters set out a considerable
part of our escort became allarmed and returned. 28 men and three
women only continued with us. After eating and suffering the
horses to graize about 2 hours we renued our march and towards
evening arrived at the lower part of the cove. Shields killed an
antelope on the way a part of which we took and gave the remainder to the Indians. Being now informed of the place at which I
expected to meat Capt. C. and the party they insisted on making a
halt, which was complyed with.

We now dismounted and the chief with much cerimony put
tippets about our necks such as they themselves woar. I redily perceived that this was to disguise us and owed it's origine to the same
cause already mentioned. To give them further confidence I put
my cocked hat with feather on the chief and my over shirt being of
the Indian form my hair deshivled and skin well browned with the
sun I wanted no further addition to make me a complete Indian in
appearance.

We now set out and rode briskly within sight of the forks making one of the Indians carry the flag that our own party should
know who we were. When we arrived in sight at the distance of

about 2 miles I discovered to my mortification that the party had not arrived, and the Indians slackened their pace. I now scarcely knew what to do and feared every moment when they would halt altogether. I now determined to restore their confidence cost what it might and therefore gave the chief my gun and told him that if his enimies were in those bushes before him that he could defend himself with that gun, that for my own part I was not affraid to die and if I deceived him he might make what uce of the gun he thought proper or in other words that he might shoot me. The men also gave their guns to other Indians which seemed to inspire them with more confidence; they sent their spies before them at some distance and when I drew near the place I thought of the notes which I had left and directed Drewyer to go with an Indian man and bring them to me which he did.

The Indian seeing him take the notes from the stake on which they had been placed. I now had recource to a stratagem in which I thought myself justifyed by the occasion, but which I must confess set a little awkward. It had it's desired effect. After reading the notes which were the same I had left I told the chief that when I had left my brother chief with the party below where the river entered the mountain that we both agreed not to bring the canoes higher up than the next forks of the river above us wherever this might happen, that there he was to wait my return, should he arrive first, and that in the event of his not being able to travel as fast as usual from the difficulty of the water, that he was to send up to the first forks above him and leave a note informing me where he was. That this note was left here today and that he informed me that he was just below the mountains and was coming on slowly up, and added that I should wait here for him, but if they did not beleive me that I should send a man at any rate to the chief and they might also send one of their young men with him, that myself and two others would remain with them at this place.

This plan was readily adopted and one of the young men offered his services; I promised him a knife and some beads as a reward for his confidence in us. Most of them seemed satisfyed but there were several that complained of the chief's exposing them to danger unnecessarily and said that we told different stories. In short a few were much dissatisfyed. I wrote a note to Capt. Clark by the light of some willow brush and directed Drewyer to set out early being confident that there was not a moment to spare.

The chief and five or six others slept about my fire and the others hid themselves in various parts of the willow brush to avoid the enemy whom they were fearfull would attack them in the course of the night. I now entertained various conjectures myself with rispect to the cause of Capt. Clarks detention and was even fearfull that he had found the river so difficult that he had halted below the Rattlesnake bluffs. I knew that if these people left me that they would immediately disperse and secrete themselves in the mountains where it would be impossible to find them or at least in vain to pursue them and that they would spread the allarm to all other bands within our reach & of course we should be disappointed in obtaining horses, which would vastly retard and increase the labour of our voyage and I feared might so discourage the men as to defeat the expedition altogether.

My mind was in reallity quite as gloomy all this evening as the most affrighted indian but I affected cheerfullness to keep the Indians so who were about me. We finally laid down and the chief placed himself by the side of my musquetoe bier. I slept but little as might be well expected, my mind dwelling on the state of the expedition which I have ever held in equal estimation with my own existence, and the fait of which appeared at this moment to depend in a great measure upon the caprice of a few savages who are ever as fickle as the wind. I had mentioned to the chief several times that we had with us a woman of his nation who had been taken prisoner by the Minnetares, and that by means of her I hoped to explain myself more fully than I could do signs.

Some of the party had also told the Indians that we had a man with us who was black and had short curling hair. This had excited their curiossity very much and they seemed quite as anxious to see this monster as they were the merchandise which we had to barter for their horses.

[Lewis] August 17, 1805

This morning I arrose very early and dispatched Drewyer and the Indian down the river. Drewyer had been gone about 2 hours when an Indian who had straggled some little distance down the river returned and reported that the whitemen were coming, that he had seen them just below. They all appeared transported with joy, & the chief repeated his fraturnal hug. I felt quite as much gratified at this information as the Indians appeared to be. Shortly after Capt. Clark arrived with the interpreter Charbono, and the Indian woman, who proved to be a sister of the Chief Cameah-walt. The meeting of those people was really affecting, particularly between Sah-cah-gar-we-ah and an Indian woman, who had been taken prisoner at the same time with her and who, had afterwards escaped from the Minnetares and rejoined her nation.

At noon the canoes arrived, and we had the satisfaction once more to find ourselves all together, with a flattering prospect of being able to obtain as many horses shortly as would enable us to prosicute our voyage by land should that by water be deemed unadvisable.

The chief thanked us for friendship towards himself and nation & declared his wish to serve us in every rispect. That he was sorry to find that it must yet be some time before they could be furnished with firearms but said they could live as they had done heretofore untill we brought them as we had promised. He said they had not horses enough with them at present to remove our baggage to their village over the mountains but that he would return tomorrow and encourage his people to come over with their horses and that he would bring his own and assist us.

We gave the chief an uniform coat shirt a pair of scarlet legings a carrot of tobacco and some small articles to each of the others we gave a shirt legings handkerchief a knife some tobacco and a few small articles we also distributed a good quantity paint, mockerson, awles, knives, beads, looking-glasses &c. among the other Indians and gave them a plentifull meal of lyed (hull taken of by being boiled in lye) corn which was the first they had ever eaten in their lives. They were much pleased with it. Every article about us appeared to excite astonishment in ther minds. The appearance of the men, their arms, the canoes, our manner of working them, the black man York and the sagacity of my dog were equally objects of admiration.

I also shot my air-gun which was so perfectly incomprehensible that they immediately denominated it the great medicine. The idea which the Indians mean to convey by this appellation is something that eminates from or acts immediately by the influence or power of the great sperit; or that, in which, the power of god is manifest by it's incomprehensible power of action. Our hunters killed 4 deer and an antelope this evening of which we also gave the Indians a good proportion. The ceremony of our council and smoking the pipe was in conformity of the custom of this nation performed bearfoot. On those occasions points of etiquet are quite as much attended to by the Indians as among scivilized nations. To keep indians in a good humour you must not fatiegue them with too much business at one time.

[Lewis] August 18, 1805

This day I completed my thirty first year, and conceived that I had in all human probability now existed about half the period which I am to remain in this sublunary world. I reflected that I

had as yet done but little, very little, indeed, to further the hapiness
of the human race, or to advance the information of the succeeding
generation. I viewed with regret the many hours I have spent in
indolence, and now soarly feel the want of that information which
those hours would have given me had they been judiciously
expended. But since they are past and cannot be recalled, I dash
from me the gloomy thought, and resolved in future, to redouble
my exertions and at least indeavour to promote those two primary
objects of human existence, by giving them the aid of that portion
of talents which nature and fortune have bestoed on me; or in
future, to live *for mankind*, as I have heretofore lived *for myself*.

[Lewis] August 19, 1805

The frost which perfectly whitened the grass this morning had a
singular appearance to me at this season. This evening I made a few
of the men construct a sein of willow brush which we hawled and
caught a large number of fine trout . . . the trout are the same which
I first met with at the falls of the Missouri. They are larger than the
speckled trout of our mountains and equally as well flavored.

From what has been said of the Shoshones it will be readily perceived that they live in a wretched stait of poverty. Yet notwithstanding their extreem poverty they are not only cheerfull but even
gay, fond of gaudy dress and amusements; like most other Indians
they are great egotists and frequently boast of heroic acts which
they never performed. They are also fond of games of wrisk. They
are frank, communicative, fair in dealing, generous with the little
they possess, extreemly honest, and by no means beggarly. Each
individual is his own sovereign master, and acts from the dictates
of his own mind; the authority, of the cheif being nothin more than
mere admonition supported by the influence which the propriety
of his own exemplary conduct may have acquired him in the
minds of the individuals who compose the band.

The title of cheif is not hereditary, nor can I learn that there is any cerimony of instalment, or other epoch in the life of a cheif from which his title as such can be dated. In fact everyman is a chief, but all have not an equal influence on the minds of the other members of the community, and he who happens to enjoy the greatest share of confidence is the principal chief.

The Shoshonees may be estimated at about 100 warriors, and about three times that number of women and children. They have more children among them than I expected to have seen among a people who procure subsistence with such difficulty. There are but few very old persons, nor did they appear to treat those with much tenderness or rispect. The man is the sole propryetor of his wives and daughters, and can barter or dispose of either as he thinks proper. A plurality of wives is common among them, but these are not generally sisters as with the Minnitares & Mandans but are purchased of different fathers. The father frequently disposes of his infant daughters in marriage to men who are grown or to men who have sons for whom they think proper to provide wives. The compensation given in such cases usually consists of horses or mules which the father receives at the time of contract and converts to his own uce. The girl remains with her parents untill she is conceived to have obtained the age of puberty which with them is considered to be about the age of 13 or 14 years. The female at this age is surrendered to her soverlegn lord and husband agreeably to contract, and with her is frequently restored by the father quite as much as he received in the first instance in payment for his daughter; but this is discretionary with the father. Sah-car-gar-we-ah had been thus disposed of before she was taken by the Minnetares, or had arrived to the years of puberty. The husband was yet living with this band. He was more than double her age and had two other wives. He claimed her as his wife but said that as she had had a child by another man, who was Charbono, that he did not want her.

They seldom correct their children particularly the boys who soon become masters of their own acts. They give as a reason that it cows and breaks the sperit of the boy to whip him, and that he never recovers his independence of mind after he is grown. They treat their women but with little rispect, and compel them to perform every species of drudgery. They collect the wild fruits and roots, attend to the horses or assist in that duty, cook, dress the skins and make all their apparel, collect wood and make their fires, arrange and form their lodges, and when they travel pack the horses and take charge of all the baggage. In short the man dose little else except attend his horses, hunt and fish. The man considers himself degraded if he is compelled to walk any distance; and if he is so unfortunately poor as only to possess two horses he rides the best himself and leavs the woman or women if he has more than one, to transport their baggage and children on the other, and to walk if the horse is unable to carry the additional weight of their persons.

The chastity of their women is not held in high estimation, and the husband will for a trifle barter the companion of his bead for a night or longer if he conceives the reward adiquate; tho' they are not so importunate that we should caress their women as the Siouxs were. And some of their women appear to be held more sacred than in any nation we have seen. I have requested the men to give them no cause of jealousy by having connection with their women without their knowledge, which with them, strange as it may seem is considered as disgracefull to the husband, as clandestine connections of a similar kind are among civilized nations. To prevent this mutual exchange of good officies altogether I know it impossible to effect, particularly on the part of our young men whom some months abstanence have made very polite to those tawney damsels. No evil has yet resulted and I hope will not from these connections. . . .

I was anxious to learn whether these people had the venerial, and made the enquiry through the intrepreter and his wife; the information was that they sometimes had it but I could not learn their remedy; they most usually die with it's effects. This seems a strong proof that these disorders bothe ganaraehah [gonorrhea] and Louis Venerae are native disorders of America.

[Lewis] August 20, 1805

The tippet of the Snake Indians is the most elegant peice of Indian dress I ever saw. The neck or collar of this is formed of a strip of dressed otter skin with the fur. It is about four or five inches wide and is cut out of the back of the skin the nose and eyes forming one extremity and the tall the other. Beginning a little behind the ear of the animal at one edge of this collar and proceeding towards the tail, they attach from one to two hundred and fifty little roles of ermin skin . . . they are confined at the upper point in little bundles of two, three, or more as the disign may be to make them more full; these are then attatched to the collars as before mentioned, and to conceal the connection of this part which would otherwise have a course appearance they attach a broad fringe of the ermin skin to the collar overlaying that part. Little bundles of fine fringe of the same materials is fastened to the extremity of the tails in order to shew their black extremities to greater advantage. The center of the otterskin collar is also ornamented with the shells of the perl oister. The collar is confined around the neck and the little roles of ermin skin about the size of a large quill covers the solders and body nearly to the waist and has the appearance of a short cloak and is really handsome.

[Lewis] August 20, 1805

I now prevailed on the chief to instruct me with rispect to the geography of his country. This he undertook very cheerully, by delienating the rivers on the ground. But I soon found that his information fell far short of my expectation or wishes. He drew the river on which we now are [i.e., Lemhi] to which he placed two branches just above us, which he shewed me from the openings of the mountains were in view. He next made it discharge itself into a large river which flowed from the S.W. about ten miles below us, then continued this joint stream in the same direction of this valley or N.W. for one days march and then enclined it to the west for 2 more days march. Here he placed a number of heaps of sand on each side which he informed me represented the vast mountains of rock eternally covered with snow through which the river passed. That the perpendicular and even juting rocks so closely hemned in the river that there was no possibility of passing along the shore; that the bed of the river was obstructed by sharp pointed rocks and the rapidity of the stream such that the whole surface of the river was beat into perfect foam as far as the eye could reach. That the mountains were also inaccessible to man or horse.

He said that this being the state of the country in that direction that himself nor none of his nation had ever been further down the river than these mountains. I then enquired the state of the country on either side of the river but he could not inform me. He said there was an old man of his nation a days march below who could proba-bly give me some information of the country to the N.W. and refered me to an old man then present for that to the S.W. The chief further informed me that he had understood from the Persed Nosed Indi-ans[9] who inhabit this river below the rocky mountains that it ran a great way toward the seting sun and finally lost itself in a great lake of water which was illy taisted, and where the white men lived. I next commenced my enquiries of the old man to whom I had been refered for information relative the country S.W. of us. This he depicted with horrors and obstructions scarcely inferior to that just mentioned. He informed me that the band of this nation to which he belonged resided at the distance of 20 days march from hence not far from the white people with whom they traded for horses mules cloth

metal beads and the shells which they woar as orniment being those
of a species of perl oister. That the course to his relations was a little
to the west of south. That in order to get to his relations the first
seven days we should be obliged to climb over steep and rocky
mountains where we could find no game to kill nor anything but
roots such as a ferce and warlike nation lived on whom he called the
broken mockersons or mockersons with holes, and said inhabited
those mountains and lived like the bear of other countries among the
rocks and fed on roots or the flesh of such horses as they could take
or steel from those who passed through their country. That in passing this country the feet of our horses would be so much wounded
with the stones many of them would give out. The next part of the
rout was about 10 days through a dry and parched sandy desert in
which [there is] no food at this season for either man or horse, and in
which we must suffer if not perish for the want of water. That the
sun had now dryed up the little pools of water which exist through
this desert plain in the spring season and had also scorched all the
grass. That no animal inhabited this plain on which we could hope to
subsist. That about the center of this plain a large river passed from
S.E. to N.W. which was navigable but afforded neither salmon nor
timber. That beyond this plain three or four days march his relations
lived in a country tolerable fertile and partially covered with timber on
another large river which ran in the same direction of the former. That
this last discharged itself into a large river on which many numerous
nations lived with whom his relations were at war but whether this
last discharged itself into the great lake or not he did not know.

I now asked Cameahwait by what rout the Pierced Nosed Indians, who he informed me inhabited this river below the mountains,
came over to the Missouri; this he informed me was to the north, but
added that the road was a very bad one as he had been informed by
them and that they had suffered excessively with hunger on the rout
being obliged to subsist for many days on berries alone as there was

no game in that part of the mountains which were broken rockey and so thickly covered with timber that they could scarcely pass. However knowing that Indians had passed, and did pass, at this season on that side of this river to the same below the mountains, my rout was instantly settled in my own mind. . . . I felt perfectly satisfyed, that if the Indians could pass these mountains with their women and children, that we could also pass them.

---

1. The Judith River, at first named "Bighorn" by Lewis, was afterward renamed by Clark in honor of Julia Hancock of Fincastle, Virginia, who later became his wife. She was but thirteen years old at this time, and was nicknamed Judy by her friends. —Ed.

2. A variety of the common red fox, known as the cross-fox. —Ed.

3. Miss Maria Wood, a cousin of Lewis's. —Ed.

4. A reference to James Thompson, an eighteenth-century Scottish poet and author of *The Seasons*. —Ed.

5. They were cutthroat trout, *Salmo clarkii*, so named in honor of Clark. —LYJ

6. Possibly this was a wolverine; may have been a cougar. —Ed.

7. Lewis was at Lemhi Pass, on the border between Montana and Idaho. When he and his men crossed the border, they became the first U.S. citizens to cross the Continental Divide. —LYJ

8. This was the Lemhi River, whose waters at last find their way into the Columbia. —Ed.

9. Commonly known as Nez Perce, also named Chopunish; they were the largest branch of the Shahaptian stock, whose tribes occupied a large area on the Columbia and its tributaries in Idaho and eastern Oregon. —Ed.

VOLUME THREE

FROM THE SHOSHONI CAMP ON LEMHI RIVER TO FORT CLATSOP

August 21, 1805–January 9, 1806

[Lewis] August 21, 1805

This morning was very cold. The ice ¼ of an inch thick on the water which stood in the vessels exposed to the air. Some wet deerskins that had been spread on the grass last evening are stiffly frozen. The ink freizes in my pen. . . .

The warriors or such as esteem themselves brave men wear collars made of the claws of the brown bear which are also esteemed of great value and are preserved with great care. It is esteemed by them an act of equal celebrity the killing one of these bear or an enimy, and with the means they have of killing this animal it must really be a serious undertaking.

The guide appeared to be a very friendly intelligent old man. Capt. C. is much pleased with him.

[Lewis] August 22, 1805

Late last night Drewyer returned with a fawn he had killed and a considerable quantity of Indian plunder. The anecdote with rispect to the latter is perhaps worthy of relation. He informed me that while hunting in the Cove yesterday about 12 o'clock he came suddonly upon an Indian Camp, at which there were a young man an old man and a boy and three women, that they seemed but little supprised at seeing him and he rode up to them and dismounted turning [his] horse out to graize. These people had just finished their repast on some roots. He entered into conversation with them by signs, and after about 20 minutes one of the women spoke to the others of the party and they all went immediately and collected their horses brought them to camp and saddled them. At this moment he thought he would also set out and continue his hunt, and accordingly walked to catch his horse at some little distance and neglected to take up his gun which he left at camp.

The Indians perceiving him at the distance of fifty paces immediately mounted their horses, the young man took the gun, and the whole of them left their baggage and laid whip to their horses directing their course to the pass of the mountains. Finding himself deprived of his gun he immediately mounted his horse and pursued. After runing them about 10 miles the horses of two of the women nearly gave out and the young fellow with the gun from their frequent crys slackened his pace and being on a very fleet horse road around the women at a little distance. At length Drewer overtook the women and by signs convinced them that he did not wish to hirt them. They then halted and the young fellow approached still nearer. He asked him for his gun but the only part of the answer which he could understand was Pahkee which he knew to be the name by which they called their enemies.

Watching his opportunity when the fellow was off his guard he suddonly rode along side of him seized his gun and wrested her out of his hands. The fellow finding Drewyer too strong for him and discovering that he must yeald the gun had presents of mind to open the pan and cast the priming before he let the gun escape from his hands; now finding himself devested of the gun he turned his horse about and laid whip, leaving the women to follow him as well as they could. Drewyer now returned to the place they had left their baggage and brought it with him to my camp.

[Lewis] August 23, 1805

The Indians pursued a mule buck near our camp. I saw this chase for about 4 miles. It was really entertaining. There were about twelve of them in pursuit of it on horseback, they finally rode it down and killed it. They all came in about 1 p.m. having killed 2 mule deer and three goats. This mule buck was the largest deer of any kind I had ever seen. It was nearly as large as a doe elk. I observed that there was but little division or distribution of the meat they had taken among themselves. Some familes had a large stock and others none. This is not customary among the nations of Indians with whom I have hitherto been acquainted.

I asked Cameahwait the reason why the hunters did not divide the meat among themelves. He said that meat was so scarce with them that the men who killed it reserved it for themselves and their own families. My hunters arrived about 2 in the evening with two mule deer and three common deer. I distributed three of the deer among those families who appeared to have nothing to eat.

The next morning Lewis, Cameahwait, and their men left Camp Fortunate, at the fork of the Beaverhead, and began a ride west to rejoin Cameahwait's tribe at Lemhi Pass.

[Lewis] August 24, 1805

I had now the inexpressible satisfaction to find myself once more under way with all my baggage and party. An Indian had the politeness to offer me one of his horses to ride which I accepted with cheerfulness as it enabled me to attend better to the march of the party . . .

Cameahwait literally translated is *one who never walks*. He told me that his nation had also given him another name by which he was signalized as a warrior which was Too-et'-te-can'-e or *black gun*. These people have many names in the course of their lives, particularly if they become distinguished characters. For it seems that every important event by which they happen to distinguish themselves intitles them to claim another name which is generally scelected by themselves and confirmed by the nation. Those distinguishing acts are the killing and scalping an enemy, the killing a white bear, leading a party to war who happen to be successfull either in destroying their enemies or robing them of their horses, or individually stealing the horses of an enemy.

These are considered acts of equal heroism among them, and that of killing an enemy without scalping him is considered of no importance. In fact the whole honour seems to be founded in the act of scalping, for if a man happens to slay a dozen of his enemies in action and others get the scalps or first lay their hand on the dead person the honor is lost to him who killed them and devolves on those who scalp or first touch them.

Among the Shoshones, as well as all the Indians of America, bravery is esteemed the primary virtue; nor can any one become eminent among them who has not at some period of his life given proofs of his possessing this virtue. With them there can be no preferment without some warlike achievement, and so completely interwoven is this principle with the earliest elements of thought that it will in my opinion prove a serious obstruction to the restoration of a general peace among the nations of the Missouri.

[Lewis] August 26, 1805

One of the women who had been assisting in the transportation of the baggage halted at a little run about a mile behind us, and sent on the two pack horses which she bad been conducting by one of her female friends. I enquired of Cameahwait the cause of her detention, and was informed by him in an unconcerned manner that she had halted to bring fourth a child and would soon over-take us. In about an hour the woman arrived with her newborn babe and passed us on her way to the camp apparently as well as she ever was.

It appears to me that the facility and ease with which the women of the aborigines of North America bring fourth their children is reather a gift of nature than depending as some have supposed on the habitude of carrying heavy burthens on their backs while in a state of pregnacy. If a pure and dry air, an eliv-ated and cold country is unfavourable to childbirth, we might expect every difficult incident to that operation of nature in this part of the continent; again as the snake Indians possess an abundance of horses, their women are seldom compelled like those in other parts of the continent to carry burthens on their backs, yet they have their children with equal convenience, and it is a rare occurrence for any of them to experience difficulty in childbirth.

I have been several times informed by those who were conver-gent with the fact, that the Indian women who are pregnant by whitemen experience more difficulty in childbirth than when pregnant by an Indian.

Led by an Indian guide they called Old Toby, the captains now embarked on what turned out to be the most demanding part of their journey, the descent into the Bitterroot Valley and then the crossing of the Bitterroot Mountains on the Lolo Trail.

[Clark] September 2, 1805

Proceeded up a West fork [of Fish Creek][1] without a roade proceded on thro' thickets in which we were obliged to cut a road, over rockey hill sides where our horses were in perpeteal danger of slipping to their certain destruction & up & down steep hills, where several horses fell, some turned over, and others sliped down steep hill sides, one horse crippeled & 2 gave out. with the greatest dificuelty risque &c. we made five miles. . . .

[Clark] September 3, 1805

In the after part of the day the high mountains closed the creek on each side and obliged us to take on the steep sides of those mountains, so steep that the horses could scur[ce]lly keep from slipping down, several sliped & injured themselves verry much. . . . The mountains (we had passed) to the east covered with snow. We met with a great misfortune, in haveing our last thmometer broken, by accident. This day we passed over emence hils and some of the worst roads that ever horses passed, our horses frequently fell snow about 2 inches deep when it began to rain which termonated in a sleet [storm].

[Clark] September 4, 1805

A verry cold morning. Everything wet and frosed. Prosued our course down the creek to the forks about 5 miles where we met a party of the Tushepau [Salish, or "Flathead"] nation of 33 lodges—about 80 men, 400 total, and at least 500 horses. Those people receved us friendly, threw white robes over our sholders & smoked in the pipes of peace. We encamped with them & found them friendly but nothing but berries to eate, a part of which they gave us.

Those Indians are well dressed with skin shirts & robes, they [are] stout & light complected, more so than common for Indians. The chief harangued untill late at night, smoked in our pipe and appeared satisfied. I was the first white man who ever wer on the waters of this river.[2]

The party proceeded north in the Bitterroot Valley, making a camp they called Travellers Rest at the mouth of Lolo Creek, before turning west to cross the mountains.

[Lewis] September 10, 1805

This evening one of our hunters [Colter] returned accompanyed by three men of the Flathead nation whom he had met in his excurtion up Travellers Rest Creek. On first meeting him the Indians were alarmed and prepared for battle with their bows and arrows, but he soon relieved their fears by laying down his gun and advancing towards them. The Indians were mounted on very fine horses of which the Flatheads have a great abundance; that is, each man in the nation possesses from 20 to a hundred head. Our guide could not speake the language of these people but soon engaged them in conversation by signs or jesticulation, the common language of all the aborigines of North America, it is one understood by all of them and appears to be sufficiently copious to convey with a degree of certainty the outlines of what they wish to communicate.

[Clark] September 14, 1805

I could see no fish, and the grass entirely eaten out by the horses, we proceeded on 2 miles & encamped opposit a small island at the mouth of a branch on the right side of the river which is at this place 80 yards wide, swift and stoney. Here we were compelled to kill a colt for our men & selves to eat for the want of meat & we named the south fork Colt Killed Creek, and this river we call Flat Head River. The flat head name is *Koos koos ke*.[3] The mountains which we passed to day much worst than yesterday the last excessively bad & thickly strowed with falling timber & pine spruce fur hackmatak & tamerack, 2 steep & stoney our men and horses much fatigued.

[Clark] September 15, 1805

Several horses sliped and roled down steep hills which hurt them verry much. The one which carried my desk & small trunk turned over & roled down a mountain for 40 yards & lodged against a tree, broke the desk. The horse escaped and appeared but little hurt some others verry much hurt. From this point I observed a range of high mountains covered with snow from S.E. to S.W. with their tops bald or void of timber. After two hours delay we proceeded on up the mountain steep & ruged as usial. More timber near the top. When we arrived at the top as we conceved, we could find no water and concluded to camp and make use of the snow we found on the top to cook the remn' of our colt & make our supe, evening verry cold and cloudy. Two of our horses gave out, pore and too much hurt to proceed on and left in the rear. Nothing killed to day except 2 phest [*pheasant*].

From this mountain I could observe high ruged mountains in every direction as far as I could see. With the greatest exertion we could only make 12 miles up the mountain (*and encamped on the top of the mountain near a bank of old snow about 3 feet deep lying on the northern side of the mountain and in small banks on the top & leavel parts of the mountain. We melted the snow to drink, and cook our horseflesh to eat*).

[Clark] September 16, 1805

Began to snow about 3 hours before day and continued all day the snow in the morning 4 inches deep on the old snow, and by night we found it from 6 to 8 inches deep. I walked in front to keep the road and found great dificuelty in keeping it as in maney places the snow had entirely filled up the track . . . we are continually covered with snow. I have been wet and as cold in every part as I ever was in my life. Indeed I was at one time fearfull my feet would freeze in the thin mockirsons which I wore.

To describe the road of this day would be a repition of yesterday except the snow which made it much worse.

[Clark] September 18, 1805

Encamped opn a bold running creek passing to the left which I call *Hungery* Creek as at that place we had nothing to eate.

[Lewis] September 19, 1805

The road was excessively dangerous along this creek being a narrow rockey path generally on the side of a steep precipice, from what in many places if either man or horse were precipated they would inevitably be dashed in pieces. Fraziers horse fell from this road in the evening, and roled with his load near a hundred yards into the creek. We all expected that the horse was killed but to our astonishment when the load was taken off him he arose to his feet & appeared to be but little injured. This was the most wonderfull escape I ever witnessed.

[Clark] September 20, 1805

At 12 miles descended the mountain to a leavel pine countrey. Proceeded on through a butifull countrey for three miles to a small plain in which I found main Indian lodges. Those people gave us a small piece of buffalow meat, some dried salmon beries & roots. . . . They also gave us the bread made of this root, all of which we eate hartily. . . . They call themselves *Cho pun-nish* or *Pierced noses.*[4]

I find myself very unwell all the evening from eateing the fish & roots too freely.

[Lewis] September 21, 1805

I find myself growing weak from the want of food and most of the men complain of a similar deficiency, and have fallen off very much.

[Clark] September 21, 1805

I am verry sick to day and puke which relive me.

[Clark] September 22, 1805

The planes appeared covered with spectators viewing the white men and the articles which we had. Our party weakened and much reduced in flesh as well as strength.

[Clark, first draft] September 24, 1805

Capt. Lewis sick. All complain of a lax & heaviness at the stomak. I gave rushes pills to several.

[Clark] September 24, 1805

Capt. Lewis scercely able to ride on a jentle horse which was furnished by the chief. Several men so unwell that they were compelled to lie on the side of the road for some time. Others obliged to be put on horses. I gave Rushes pills to the sick this evening.

[Clark] September 26, 1805

Capt. Lewis still very unwell. Several men taken sick on the way down. I administered *salts* pils, galip [jalap], tarter, emetic &etc. I feel unwell this evening.

[Clark] September 27, 1805

All the men able to work commenced building 5 canoes. Several taken sick at work. Our hunters returned sick without meet.

[Clark] October 1, 1805

Nothin to eate except a little dried fish which the men complain of as working of them as *(as much as)* a dost of salts. Capt. Lewis getting much better.

[Clark] October 9, 1805

At dark we were informed that our old guilde & his son had left us and had been seen running up the river several miles above. We could not account for the cause of his leavening us at this time, without receiving his pay for the services he had rendered us, or letting us know anything of his intention.

[Clark] October 10, 1805

A miss understanding took place between Shabono one of our interpreters and Jo & R Fields which appears to have originated in just [jest]. Our diet extremely bad haveing nothing but roots and dried fish to eate. All the party have greatly the advantage of me, in as much as they all relish the flesh of the dogs, several of which we purchased of the nativs for to add to our store of fish and roots.

Incapacitated for nearly two weeks, the captains finally recovered from the effects of the Nez Perce diet and paddled their canoes up the Clearwater and then Snake rivers for the final push to the sea.

[Clark] October 14, 1805

At 12 miles we came too at the head of a rapid which the Indians told me was verry bad. We viewed the rapid [and] found it bad in decending. Three stern canoes stuck fast for some time on the head of the rapid and one struck a rock in the worst part, fortunately all landed safe below the rapid which was nearly 3 miles in length. Here we dined, and for the first time for three weeks past I had a good dinner of blue wing teel.

After dinner we set out and had not proceded on two miles before our stern canoe in passing thro a short rapid opposit the head of an island run on a smothe rock and turned broad side. The men got out on the [rock] all except one of our Indian chiefs who swam on shore.

The canoe filed and sunk. A number of articles floated out, such as the mens bedding, clothes & skins, the greater part of which were cought by 2 of the canoes, whilst a 3rd was unloading & sterning the swift current to the relief of the men on the rock, who could with much dificuelty hold the canoe. However in about an hour we got the men and canoe to shore with the loss of some bedding, tomahawks, shot pouches, skins, clothes &c. &c.

In this island we found some spilt [split] timber the parts of a house which the Indians had verry securely covered with stone. We also observed a place where the Indians had buried their fish. We have made it a point at all times not to take any thing belonging to the Indians even their wood. But at this time we are compelled to violate that rule and take a part of the split timber we find here buried for fire wood, as no other is to be found in any direction.

[Clark] October 17, 1805

The number of dead salmon on the shores & floating in the river is incrediable to say—and at this season they have only to collect the fish, split them open and dry them on their scaffolds on which they have great number . . . great numbers of Indians on the banks viewing me and 18 canoes accompanied me from the point. The waters of this river is clear, and a salmon may be seen at the deabth of 15 or 20 feet . . . passed three large lodges on the stard. side near which great number of salmon was drying on scaffolds.

One of those mat lodges I entered found it crouded with men women and children and near the enterance of those houses I saw maney squars engaged [in] splitting and drying salmon. I was furnished with a mat to set on, and one man set about prepareing me something to eate. First he brought in a piece of a drift log of pine and with a wedge of the elkshorn, and a malet of stone curioesly carved. He split the log into small pieces and lay'd it open on the fire on which he put round stones. A woman handed him a basket of water and a large salmon about half dried. When the stones were hot he put them into the basket of water with the fish which was soon sufficently boiled for use it was then taken out put on a platter of rushes neetly made, and set before me they boiled a salmon for each of the men with me.

The dress of those natives differ but little from those on the Koskoskia and Lewis's rivers, except the women who dress verry different, in as much as those above ware long leather shirts which [are] highly ornamented with beeds, shells &c. &c. and those on the main Columbia River only ware a truss or pece of leather tied around them at their hips and drawn tite between ther legs and fastened before so as barely to hide those parts which are so sacredly bid & secured by our women. Those women are more inclined to corpulency than any we have yet seen, with low stature, broad faces, heads flatened and the foward [forehead] compressed so as to form a streight line from the nose to the crown of the head. Their eyes are of a duskey black, their hair of a corse black without ornaments of any kind, braded as above . . . they take a greater share [in the] labor of the woman, than is common among savage tribes, and as I am informed [are] content with one wife (as also those on the Ki-moo-e-nim River).

Those people respect the aged with veneration. I observed an old woman in one of the lodges which I entered. She was entirely blind as I was informed by signs, had lived more than 100 winters. She occupied the best position in the house, and when she spoke great attention was paid to what she said.

[Clark] October 19, 1805

While setting on a rock wateing for Capt. Lewis I shot a crain which was flying over of the common kind. I observed a great number of lodges on the opposit side at some distance below, and several Indians on the opposit bank passing up to where Capt. Lewis was with the canoes. . . . I was fearfull that those people might not be informed of us. . . . I landed in front of five lodges which was at no great distance from each other. . . . I approached one with a pipe in my hand. Entered a lodge which was the nearest to me found 32 persons men, women and a few children setting permiscuisly in the lodge, in the greatest agutation, some crying and ringing there hands, others hanging their heads.

I gave my hand to them all and made signs of my friendly disposition and offered the men my pipe to smok and distributed a fiew small articles which I had in my pockets. This measure passified those distressed people verry much. I then sent one man into each lodge and entered a second myself. The inhabitants of which I found more fritened than those of the first lodge. I destributed sundrey small articles amongst them, and smoked with the men. I then entered the third 4th & fifth lodge which I found somewhat passified, the three men, Drewer Jo. & R. Fields, haveing useed everey means in their power to convince them of our friendly disposition to them.

I then set my self on a rock and made signs to the men to come and smoke with me. Not one come out untill the canoes arrived with the 2 chiefs, one of whom spoke aloud, and as was their custom to all we had passed. The Indians came out & set by me and smoked. They said we came from the clouds &c. &c. and were not men[5] &c. &c.

This time Capt. Lewis came down with the canoes in which the Indian[s were]. As soon as they saw the squar wife of the interperter they pointed to her and informed those who continued yet in the same position I first found them. They imediately all came out and appeared to assume new life. The sight of this Indian woman, wife to one of our interprs. confirmed those people of our friendly intentions, as no woman ever accompanies a war party of Indians in this quarter.

[Clark] October 22, 1805

Here I beheld an emence body of water compressd in a narrow chanel of about 200 yds in width, fomeing over rocks maney of which presented their tops above the water. When Capt. Lewis joined me haveing delayed on the way at this plac to examine a root of which the nativs had been digging great quanities in the bottoms of this river.... We landed and walked down accompanied by an old man to view the falls,[6] and the best rout for to make a portage.... We turned droped down to the head of the rapids and took every article except the canoes across the portag[e] where I had formed a camp on [an] ellegable situation for the protection of our stores from theft, which we were more fearfull of than their arrows. We despatched two men to examine the river on the opposit side, and [they] reported that the canoes could be taken down a narrow chanel on the opposit side after a short portage at the head of the falls, at which place the Indians take over their canoes. Indians assisted us over the portage with our heavy articles on their horses....

[Clark] October 23, 1805

I with the greater part of the men crossed in the canoes to opposit side above the falls and hauled them across the portage of 457 yards which is on the larboard side and certainly the best side the pass the canoes.... At this point we were obliged to let the canoes down by strong ropes of elk skin which we had for the purpose. One canoe in passing this place got loose by the cords breaking, and was cought by the Indians below. I accomplished this necessary business and landed safe with all the canoes at our camp below the falls by 3 oClock p.m. nearly covered with flees which were so thick amongst the straw and fish skins at the upper part of the portage ... that every man of the party was obliged to strip naked dureing the time of takeing over the canoes, that they might have an oppertunity of brushing the fleas off their legs and bodies.

We purchased 8 small fat dogs for the party to eate; the nativs not being fond of selling their good dish, compells us to make use of dog meat for food, the flesh of which the most of the party have become fond of. . . .

[Clark] October 24, 1805

Capt. Lewis and three men crossed the river and on the opposit side to view the falls which not yet taken a full view of. At 9 oClock a.m. I set out with the party and proceeded on down a rapid stream. . . . Here a tremendious black rock presented itself high and steep appearing to choke up the river; nor could I see where the water passed further than the current was drawn with a great velocity to the lar' side of this rock at which place I heard a great roreing. I landed at the lodges and the natives went with me to the top of this rock which makes from the star' side, from the top of which I could see the dificuelties we had to pass for several miles below.

At this place the water of this great river is compressed into a chanel between two rocks not exceeding forty five yards wide and continues for a ¼ of a mile when it again widens to 200 yards and continues this width for about 2 miles when it is again intersepted by rocks. This obstruction in the river accounts for the water in high floods riseing to such a hite at the last falls. The whole of the current of this great river must at all stages pass thro' this narrow chanel of 45 yards wide.[7] as the portage of our canoes over this high rock would be impossible with our strength, and the only danger in passing thro those narrows was the whorls and swills [swells] arriseing from the compression of the water, and which I thought (as also our principal watermen Peter Crusat) by good stearing we could pass down safe.

Accordingly I deturmined to pass through this place notwith-standing the horrid appearance of this agitated gut swelling, boil-ing & whorling in every direction (which from the top of the rock did not appear as bad as when I was in it); however, we passed safe to the astonishment of all the Indians of the last lodges who viewed us from the top of the rock.

The principal chief from the nation below with several of his men visited us, and afforded a favourable oppertunity of bringing about a piece and good understanding between this chief and his people and the two chiefs who accompanied us which we have the satisfaction to say we have accomplished . . . gave this great chief a medal and some other articles, of which he was much pleased. Peter Crusat played on the violin and the men danced which delighted the nativs, who shew every civility towards us.

[Clark] October 29, 1805

Here we found the chief we had seen at the long narrows. We entered his lodge and he gave us to eate pounded fish, bread made of roots, filbert nuts, & the berries of Sackecomme [*Sac de Commis*]. We gave to each woman of the lodge a brace of ribon of which they were much pleased. . . . The chief then directed his wife to hand him his medison bag which he opened and showed us 14 fingers [*different fingers not little or middle fingers*] which he said was the fingers of his enemies which he had taken in war, and pointed to S.E. from which direction I concluded they were Snake Indians.

This is the first instance I ever knew of the Indians takeing any other trofea of their exploits off the dead bodies of their enimies except the scalp. The chief painted those fingers with several other articles which was in his bag red and securely put them back, haveing first made a short harrang which I suppose was bragging of what he had done in war.

[Clark] October 31, 1805

I proceeded down the river to view with more attention [the rapids]. We had to pass on the river below. A remarkable high detached rock stands in a bottom on the star. side near the lower point [which] we call the *Beaten* [*Beacon*] *rock*.[8] One of the men shot a goose above this great shute, which was floating into the shute, when an Indian observed it plunged! into the water & swam to the goose and brought in on shore, at the head of the suck. [*great danger, rapids bad, descent close by him (150 feet of) of all Columbia River, current dashed among rocks, if he had got in the suck-lost*] As this Indian richly earned the goose I suffered him to keep it which he about half picked and spited it up with the guts in it to roste.

This great shute or falls is about ½ a mile, with the water of this great river compressed within the space of 150 paces I which there is great numbers of both large and small rock water passing with great velocity forming [foaming] & boiling in a most horriable manner.[9] . . .

[Clark] November 1, 1805

I observed in maney of the villeages which I have passed, the heads of the female children in the press for the purpose of compressing their heads in their infancy into a certain form, between two boards.

[Clark] November 4, 1805

Several canoes of Indians from the village above came down, dressed for the purpose as I supposed of paying us a friendly visit. They had scarlet & blue blankets salor jackets, overalls, shirts and hats independent of their usial dress; the most of them had either [*war axes spears or Bows sprung with quivers of arrows*] muskets or pistols and tin flasks to hold their powder. Those fellows we found assumeing and disagreeable. However we smoked with them and treated them with every attention & friendship.

Dureing the time we were at dinner those fellows stold my pipe tomahawk which they were smoking with. I imediately serched every man and the canoes, but could find nothing of my tomahawk. While serching for the tomahawk one of those scoundals stole a cappoe [*capotte* or coat] of one of our interperters, which was found stufed under the root of a tree, near the place they sat. We became much displeased with those fellows, which they discovered and moved off on their return home to their village, except 2 canoes which had passed on down.

We proceeded on [and] met a large & a small canoe from below with 12 men. The large canoe was ornamented with images carved in wood the figures of a bear in front & a man in stern, painted & fixed verry netely on the canoe, rising to near the hight of a man. Two Indians verry finely dressed & with hats on was in this canoe . . . at 3 miles lower, and 12 leagues below quick sand river passed a village of four large houses (*mulknomans*) on the lar. side, near which we had a full view of *Mt. Helien* [St. Helens] which is perhaps the highest pinical in America [*from their base*]. This is the mountain I saw from the Muscle Shell rapid on the 19th of October last covered with snow. It rises something in the form of a sugar lofe.[10]

[Clark] November 7, 1805

Great joy in camp we are in *view* of the *Ocian*, this great Pacific Octean which we been so long anxious to see. And the roreing or noise made by the waves brakeing on the rockey shores (as I suppose) maybe heard disti[n]ctly[11]

[Clark] November 8, 1805

Cloudy and disagreeable all the day. . . . Some fine rain at intervals all this day. The swells continued high all the evening & we are compelled to form an encampment on a point scercely room sufficent for us all to lie cleare of the tide water. . . . We are all wet and disagreeable, as we have been continually for several days past. We are at a loss & cannot find out if any settlement is near the mouth of this river. The swells were so high and the canoes roled in such a manner as to cause several to be verry sick. Reuben Fields, Wiser McNeal & the squar wer of the number.

[Clark] November 14, 1805

5 Indians came up in a canoe, thro the waves, which is verry high and role with great fury. They made signs to us that they saw the 3 men we sent down yesterday. Only 3 of those Indians landed, the other 2 which was women played off in the waves, which induced me to suspect that they had taken something from our men below, at this time one of the men, Colter, returned by land and informed us that those Indians had taken his gigg & basket. I called to the squars to land and give back the gigg, which they would not doe untill a man run with a gun, as if he intended to shute them when they landed, and Colter got his gig & basket. I then ordered those fellows off, and they verry readily cleared out.

Colter informed us that "it was but a short distance from where we lay around the point to a butifull sand beech, which continued for a long ways, that he had found a good harber in the mouth of a creek near 2 Indian lodges—that he had proceeded in the canoe as far as he could for the waves, the other two men Willard & Shannon had proceeded on down.["]

Capt. Lewis concluded to proceed on by land & find if possible the white people the Indians say is below and examine if a bay is situated near the mouth of this river as laid down by Vancouver in which we expect, if there is white traders to find them &c. At 3 oClock he set out with 4 men, Drewyer Jos. &Ru. Fields & R. Frasure, in one of our large canoes and 5 men to set them around the point on the sand beech. This canoe returned nearly filled with water at dark which it receved by the waves dashing into it on its return, having landed Capt. Lewis & his party safe on the sand beech. The rain continues all day. All wet. The rain &c. which has continued without a longer intermition than 2 hours at a time for ten days past has distroyd the robes and rotted nearly one half of the few clothes the party has, perticularley the leather clothes.

[Clark, first draft] November 10, 1805

Rained all the last night at intervales of sometimes of 2 hours. . . . The rainey weather continued without a longer intermition than 2 hours at a time, from the 5th in the morning untill the 16th is eleven days rain, and the most disagreeable time I have experenced confined on a tempiest coast wet, where I can neither git out to hunt, return to a better situation, or proceed on.

[Clark] November 18, 1805

I set out with 10 men and my man York to the Ocian by land. . . . and proceeded on a sandy beech . . . to a point of rocks about 40 feet high, from the top of which the hill side is open and assend with a steep assent to the tops of the mountains. . . . Here I found Capt. Lewis name on a tree. I also engraved my name, & by land the day of the month and year, as also several of the men.

[Clark] November 20, 1805

I met several parties of Chinnooks which I had not before seen, they were on their return from our camp. All those people appeared to know my deturmonation of keeping every individual of their nation at a proper distance, as they were guarded and resurved in my presence &c. found maney of the *Chin nooks* with Cap' Lewis of whome there was 2 cheifs *Com-com-mo-ly*[12] & *Chil-lar-la-wil* to whome we gave medals and to one a flag. One of the Indians had on a roab made of 2 sea otter skins the fur of them were more butifull than any fur I had ever seen. Both Capt. Lewis & my self endeavored to purchase the roab with differant articles at length we precured it for a belt of blue beeds which the squar—wife of our interpreter Shabono wore around her waste.

[Clark, first draft] November 21, 1805

The nation on the opposit side is small & called *Clap-sott*. Their great chief name Stil-la-sha. . . . Several Indians and squars came this evening I bereave for the purpose of gratifying the passions of our men. Those people appear to view sensuality as a necessary evill, and do not appear to abhore this as crime in the unmarried females. The young women sport openly with our men, and appear to receve the approbation of theer friends & relations for so doing. Maney of the women are handsome. They are all low both men and womin. I saw the name of *J. Bowmon* marked or picked on a young squars left arm.

[Clark] November 22, 1805

Before day the wind increased to a storm from the S.S.E. and blew with violence throwing the water of the river with emence waves out of its banks almost over whelming us in water. O! how horriable is the day.

[Clark] November 30, 1805

The squar gave me a piece of bread made of flour which she had reserved for her child and carefully kept untill this time, which has unfortunately got wet, and a little sour. This bread I eate with great satisfaction, it being the only mouthfull I had tasted for several months past.

[Clark] December 1, 1805

The emence seas and waves which breake on the rocks & coasts to the S.W. & N.W. roars like an emence fall at a distance, and this roaring has continued ever since our arrival in the neighbourhood of the sea coast which has been 24 days since we arrived in sight of the Great Western (for I cannot say Pacific) Ocian as I have not seen one pacific day since my arrival in its vicinity.

In December the party set about constructing their winter quarters: a log structure with palisaded walls that barely offered protection from the wind and rain. They called it Fort Clatsop, named after the nearby tribe.

[Clark] December 12, 1805

In the evening two canoes of *Clat Sops* visit us they brought with them wappato, a black sweet root they call *Sha-na-toe-qua*, and a small sea otter skin, all of which we purchased for a fiew fishing hooks and a small sack of Indian tobacco which was given [us] by the Snake Ind. Those Indians appear well disposed we gave a medal to the principal chief named *Con-ny-au* or *Com-mo-wol* and treated those with him with as much attention as we could. I can readily discover that they are close deelers, & stickle for a verry little, never close a bargin except they think they have the advantage.

[Clark] December 24, 1805

Cuscalah the Indian who had treated me so politely when I was at the Clatsops village, come up in a canoe with his young brother & 2 squars. He laid before Capt. Lewis and my self each a mat and a parcel of roots some time in the evening two files was demanded for the presents of mats and roots. As we had no files to part with, we each returned the present which we had received, which displeased Cuscalah a little. He then offered a woman to each of us which we also declined excepting of, which displeased the whole party verry much. The female part appeared to be highly disgusted at our refuseing to axcept of their favours &c.

[Clark] December 25, 1805

At day light this morning we were awoke by the discharge of the fire arms of all our party & a selute, shouts and a song which the whole party joined in under our windows, after which they retired to their rooms were chearfall all the morning. After brackfast we divided our tobacco which amounted to 12 carrots, one half of which we gave to the men of the party who used tobacco, and to those who doe not use it we make a present of a handkerchief.

The Indians leave us in the evening all the party snugly fixed in their huts. I recved a present of Capt L. of a fleece hosrie [hosiery] shirt draws and socks, a pr. mockersons of Whitehouse, a small Indian basket of Gutherich, two dozen white weazils tails of the Indian woman, & some black root of the Indians before their departure.

We would have spent this day, the nativity of Christ, in feasting, had we any thing either to raise our sperits or even gratify our appetites. Our diner concisted of pore elk, so much spoiled that we eate it thro' mear necessity. Some spoiled pounded fish and a fiew roots.

[Clark] December 31, 1805

With the party of Clatsops who visited us last was a man of much lighter coloured than the nativs are generaly. He was freckled with long duskey red hair, about 25 years of age, and must certainly be half white at least. This man seemed to understand more of the English language than the others of his party, but did not speak a word of English. He possessed all the habits of the Indians.[13]

[Lewis] January 1, 1806

This morning I was awoke at an early hour by the discharge of a volley of small arms, which were fired by our party in front of our quarters to usher in the new year. This was the only mark of rispect which we had it in our power to pay this celebrated day.

Our repast of this day tho' better than that of Christmass, consisted principally in the anticipation of the 1ˢᵗ day of January 1807, when in the bosom of our friends we hope to participate in the mirth and hilarity of the day, and when with the zest given by the recollection of the present, we shall completely, both mentally and corporally, enjoy the repast which the hand of civilization has prepared for us. At present we were content with eating our boiled elk and wappetoe, and solacing our thirst with our only beverage *pure water.*

[Clark] January 3, 1806

We were visited by our near neighbour chief or *tia Co-mo-wool* alias *Conia* and six Clapsops. They brought for sale some roots berries and 3 dogs also a small quantity of fresh blubber. This blubber they informed us they had obtained from their neighbours the *Cal-la-mox* who inhabit the coast to the S.E. Near one of their villages a whale had recently perished. This blubber the Indians eat and esteem it excellent food.

Our party from necescity have been obliged to subsist some length of time on dogs have now become extreamly fond of their flesh. It is worthey of remark that while we lived principally on the flesh of this animal we wer much more helthy strong and more fleshey then we have been sence we left the buffalow country. As for my own part I have not become reconsiled to the taste of this animal as yet.

[Lewis] January 4, 1806

Comowooll and the Clatsops who visited us yesterday left us in the evening. These people the Chinnooks and others residing in this neighbourhood and speaking the same language have been very friendly to us. They appear to be a mild inoffensive people but will pilfer if they have an opportunity to do so where they conceive themselves not liable to detection. They are great higlers in trade and if they conceive you anxious to purchase will be a whole day

bargaining for a handfull of roots. This I should have thought proceeded from their want of knowledge of the comparitive value of
articles of merchandize and the fear of being cheated, did I not
find that they invariably refuse the price first offered them and
afterwards very frequently accept a smaller quantity of the same
article. In order to satisfy myself on this subject I once offered a
Chinnook my watch two knives and a considerable quantity of
beads for a small inferior sea otter's skin which I did not much
want, he immediately conceived it of great value, and refused to
barter except I would double the quantity of beads. The next day
with a great deal of importunity on his part I received the skin in
exchange for a few strans of the same beads he had refused the day
before. I therefore believe this trait in their character proceeds
from an avaricious all grasping disposition. In this rispect they differ from all Indians I ever became acquainted with, for their dispo-
sitions invariably lead them to give whatever they are possessed off
no matter how useful or valuable, for a bauble which pleases their
fancy, without consulting it's usefullness or value.

[Lewis] January 5, 1806

Willard and Wiser returned, they had not been lost as we
apprehended. They informed us that it was not untill the fifth day
after leaving the fort that they could find a convenient place for
making salt; that they had at length established themselves on the
coast about 15 miles S.W. from this, near the lodge of some Killa-
muck families; that the Indians were very friendly and had given
them a considerable quantity of the blubber of a whale which perished on the coast some distance S.E. of them. Part of this blubber
they brought with them. It was white & not unlike the fat of poork,
tho' the texture was more spongey and somewhat coarser.

I had a part of it cooked and found it very pallitable and tender,
it resembled the beaver or the dog in flavour. It may appear some-

what extraordinary tho' it is a fact that the flesh of the beaver and dog possess a very great affinity in point of flavour. These lads also informed us that J. Fields, Bratton and Gibson (the salt makers) had with their assistance erected a comfortable camp killed an elk and several deer and secured a good stock of meat; they commenced the making of salt and found that they could obtain from 3 quarts to a gallon a day; they brought with them a specemine of the salt of about a gallon. We found it excellent, fine, strong, & white; this was a great treat to myself and most of the party, having not had any since the 20th ultmo.

I say most of the party, for my friend Capt. Clark. declares it to be a mear matter of indifference with him whether he uses it or not; for myself I must confess I felt a considerable inconvenience from the want of it; the want of bread I consider as trivial provided I get fat meat. For as to the species of meat I am not very particular. The flesh of the dog the horse and the wolf, having from habit become equally formiliar with any other, and I have learned to think that if the chord be sufficiently strong, which binds the soul and boddy together, it dose not so much matter about the materials which compose it.

[Lewis] January 6, 1806

Capt. Clark set out after an early breakfast with the party in two canoes as had been concerted the last evening. Charbono and his Indian woman were also of the party; the Indian woman was very importunate to be permited to go, and was therefore indulged. She observed that she had traveled a long way with us to see the great waters, and that now that monstrous fish was also to be seen, she thought it very hard she could not be permitted to see either (she had never yet been to the ocean).

The Clatsops, Chinnooks, Killamucks &c. are very loquacious and inquisitive; they possess good memories and have repeated to us the names capasities of the vessels &c. of many traders and others who have visited the mouth of this river. They are generally low in stature, proportionably small, reather lighter complected and much more illy formed than the Indians of the Missouri and those of our frontier. They are generally cheerfull but never gay. With us their conversation generally turns upon the subjects of trade, smoking, eating or their women; about the latter they speak without reserve in their presents, of their every part, and of the most formiliar connection. They do not hold the virtue of their women in high estimation, and will even prostitute their wives and daughters for a fishing hook or a stran of beads.

In common with other savage nations they make their women perform every species of domestic drudgery. But in almost every species of this drudgery the men also participate. Their women are also compelled to geather roots, and assist them in taking fish, which articles form much the greatest part of their subsistence; notwithstanding the survile manner in which they treat their women they pay much more rispect to their judgment and oppinions in many rispects than most indian nations. Their women are permitted to speak freely before them, and sometimes appear to command with a tone of authority. They generally consult them in their traffic and act in conformity to their opinions. I think it may be established as a general maxim that those nations treat their old people and women with most differrence [deference] and respect where they subsist principally on such articles that these can participate with the men in obtaining them; and that, that part of the community are treated with least attention, when the act of procuring subsistence devolves entirely on the men in the vigor of life. It appears to me that nature has been much more deficient in her filial tie than in any other of the strong affections of the human heart, and therefore think, our old men equally with our women indebted to civilization for their ease and comfort.

Among the Siouxs, Assinniboins and others on the Missouri who subsist by hunting, it is a custom when a person of either sex becomes so old and infirm that they are unable to travel on foot from camp to camp as they rome in surch of subsistance, for the children or near relations of such person to leave them without compunction or remorse. On these occasions they usually place within their reach a small peace of meat and a platter of water, telling the poor old super-annuated wretch for his consolation, that he or she had lived long enough, that it was time they should dye and go to their relations who can afford to take care of them much better than they could. I am informed that this custom prevails even among the Minetares, Arwaharmays and Recares when attended by their old people on their hunting excurtions; but in justice to these people I must observe that it appeared to me at their vilages, that they provided tolerably well for their aged persons, and several of their feasts appear to have principally for their object a contribution for their aged and infirm persons.

[Lewis] January 7, 1806

Last evening Drewyer visited his traps and caught a beaver and an otter. The beaver was large and fat we have therefore fared sumptuously today. This we consider a great prize for another reason. It being a full grown beaver was well supplyed with the materials for making bate with which to catch others. This bate when properly prepared will intice the beaver to visit it as far as he can smell it, and this I think may be safely stated at a mile, their sense of smelling being very accute.

To prepare beaver bate, the castor or bark stone is taken as the base. This is gently pressed out of the bladderlike bag which contains it, into a phiol of 4 ounces with a wide mouth; if you have them you will put from four to six stone in a phiol of that capacity. To this you will add half a nutmeg, a douzen or 15 grains of cloves and thirty grains of cinimon finely pulverized. Stir them well together and then add as much ardent sperits to the composition as will reduce it the consistency [of] mustard prepared for the table. When thus prepared it resembles mustard precisely to all appearance. When you cannot procure a phiol a bottle made of horn or a tight earthen vessel will answer. In all cases it must be excluded from the air or it will soon loose it's virtue.

It is fit for uce immediately it is prepared but becomes much stronger and better in about four or five days and will keep for months provided it be perfectly secluded from the air. When cloves are not to be had use double the quantity of allspice, and when no spice can be obtained use the bark of the root of sausafras when sperits can not be had use oil stone of the beaver adding mearly a sufficient quantity to moisten the other materials, or reduce it to a stif paste. It appears to me that the principal uce of the spices is only to give a variety to the scent of the bark stone and if so the mace vineller [vanilla] and other sweet smelling spices might be employed with equal advantage.

[Lewis] January 8, 1806

The Clatsops, Chinnooks and others inhabiting the coast and country in this neighbourhood, are excessively fond of smoking tobacco. In the act of smoking they appear to swallow it as they draw it from the pipe, and for many draughts together you will not perceive the smoke which they take from the pipe. In the same manner also they inhale it in their lungs untill they become surcharged with this vapour when they puff it out to a great distance through their nostrils and mouth. I have no doubt the smoke of the tobacco in this manner becomes much more intoxicating and that they do possess themselves of all it's virtues in their fullest extent; they freequently give us sounding proofs of it's creating a dismorallity of order in the abdomen, nor are those light matters thought indelicate in either sex, but all take the liberty of obeying the dictates of nature without reserve.

[Clark] January 8, 1806

We set out early and proceeded to the top of the mountain. From this point I beheld the grandest and most pleasing prospects which my eyes ever surveyed. In my frount a boundless ocean; to the N. and N.E. the coast as far as my sight could be extended; the seas rageing with emence waves and brakeing with great force from the rocks of Cape Disapointment as far as I could see to the N.W; The Clatsops, Chinnooks and other villagers on each side of the Columbia River and in the praries below me; the meanderings of 3 handsom streams heading in small lakes at the foot [of] the high country; the Columbia River for some distance up, with its bays and small rivers. And on the other side I have a view of the coast for an emence distance to the S.E. by S. the nitches and points of high land which forms this corse for a long ways aded to the inoumerable rocks of emence rise out at a great distance from the shore and against which the seas brak with great force gives this coast a most romantic appearance. . . .

I proceeded on down a steep decent to a single house the remains of an old *Kil-a-mox* Town in a nitch imediately on the sea coast, at which place great no. of eregular rocks are out and the waves comes in with great force. Near this old town I observed large canoes of the neetest kind on the ground, some of which appeared nearly decayed others quite sound. I examoned those canoes and found that [they] were the repository of the dead.

This custom of secureing the dead differs a little from the Chinnooks. The Kilamox secure the dead bodies in an oblong box of plank, which is placed in an open canoe resting on the ground, in which is put a paddle and sundery other articles the property of the disceased. The coast in the neighbourhood of this old village is slipping from the sides of the high hills, in emence masses; fifty or a hundred acres at a time give way and a great proportion of [in] an instant precipitated into the ocean. . . .

[We] proceeded to the place the whale had perished, found only the skelleton of this monster on the sand between (2 of) the villages of the *Kil-a-mox* nation; the whale was already pillaged of every valuable part by the Kilamox Inds. in the vecinity of whose village's it lay on the strand where the waves and tide had driven up & left it. This skeleton measured 105 ft.

I returned to the village of 5 cabins on the creek which I shall call *E-co-la* or Whale Creek, found the nativs busily engaged boiling the blubber, which they performed in a large squar wooden trought by means of hot stones. The oil when extracted was secured in bladders and the guts of the whale. The blubber from which the oil was only partially extracted by this process, was laid by in their cabins in large flickes [flitches] for use; those flickes they usially expose to the fire on a wooden spit untill it is prutty well wormed through and then eate it either alone or with roots of the rush, *Shaw-na-tak-we* or diped in the oil. The *Kil-a-mox* although they possessed large quantities of this blubber and oil were so prenurious that they disposed of it with great reluctiance and in small quantities only; insomuch that my utmost exertion aided by the party with the small stock of merchindize I had taken with me were notable to precure more blubber than about 300 lb. and a fiew gallons of oil; small as this stock is I prise it highly; and thank providence for directing the whale to us; and think him much more kind to us than he was to Jonah, having sent this monster to be *swallowed by us* in sted of *swallowing of us* as Jonah's did.

[Clark] January 9, 1806

Wile smokeing with the nativ's I was alarmed by a loud shrill voice from the cabins on the opposite side. The Indians all run immediately across to the village. My guide who continued with me made signs that home one's throat was cut. By enquiry I found that one man, McNeal, was absent. I imediately sent off Sergt. N. Pryor & 4 men in quest of McNeal who they met comeing across the creak in great hast, and informed me that the people were alarmed on the opposit side at something but what he could not tell. A man had verry friendly envited him to go and eate in his lodge, that the Indian had locked armes with him and went to a lodge in which a woman gave him some blubber, that the man envited him to another lodge to get something better, and the woman [*knowing his design* —Biddle] held him [*M'Neal*] by the blanket which he had around him (*He not knowing her object freed himself & was going off, when [This woman a Chinnook an old friend of M'Neals* —Biddle] and another ran out and hollow'd and his pretended friend disapeared. I emediately ordered every man to hold themselves in a state of rediness and sent Sergt. Pryor & 4 men to know the cause of the alarm which was found to be a premeditated plan of the pretended friend of McNeal to ass[ass]anate [him] for his blanket and what fiew articles he had about him, which was found out by a Chinnook woman who allarmed the men of the village who were with me in time to prevent the horred act. This man was of another band at some distance and ran off as soon as he was discovered.

I had the blubber & oil divided among the party and set out about sunrise and returned by the same rout we had went out. Met several parties of men & women of the Chinnook and Clatsops nations, on their way to trade with the *Kil-a-mox* for blubber and oil. On the steep decent of the mountain I overtook five men and six women with emence loads of the oil and blubber of the whale, those Indians had passed by some rout by which we missed them as we went out yesterday. One of the women in the act of getting down a steep part of the mountain her load by some means had sliped off her back, and she was holding the load by a strap which was fastened to the mat bag in which it was in, in one hand and holding a bush by the other. As I was in front of my party, I endeavoured to relieve this woman by takeing her load untill she could get to a better place a little below, & to my astonishment found the load as much as I could lift and must exceed 100 lbs.

---

1. Fish Creek is now known as the North Fork of the Salmon. —Ed.

2. The explorers met the Salish (or Flathead) Indians in present-day Ross' Hole, near the East Fork of the Bitterroot River.

3. Today it is known as the Clearwater.

4. Clark had found the Nez Perce tribe on today's Weippe Prairie, near Weippe, Idaho. —LYJ

5. The Biddle text explains this notion: these Indians had seen the birds which Clark had shot fall from the sky, and, connecting this with the fact that some clouds were floating above, they imagined that he had dropped from the clouds. The sound of his gun (a weapon which they had never seen), and his use of a burning-glass to make fire, confirmed their superstitious dread. —Ed.

6. Now known as Celilo Falls; at their head is the town of Celilo, Oregon. —Ed.

7. The so-called Short Narrows of the Columbia. —Ed.

8. This rock is a well-known landmark on the lower river and stands today as it did in the time of Lewis and Clark. It has been called Pillar Rock, but is now usually known as Castle Rock. —Ed.

9. This area is known as the Cascades of the Columbia, a stretch of water several miles long where the river breaks through the Cascade Mountains.

10. This was probably the explorers' first view of Mount St. Helens, which rises to an altitude of 9,750 feet in Skamania County, Washington. This peak was first sighted by Vancouver in May 1792, and named the following October, in honor of Lord St. Helens, then British ambassador at Madrid. —Ed.

11A. The ocean could not possibly be seen from this point, although during a storm the breakers might be heard. The explorers probably mistook the great bay of the river, which just below this point widens to fifteen miles, for the expanse of the ocean. —Ed.

11B. In his field journal, Clark writes *"Ocian in view! O! the joy."* — LYJ

12. A daughter of this chief became the wife (1813) of Duncan McCougal, one of the associates of John Jacob Astor. —Ed.

13. Ross Cox, in his *Adventures on the Columbia* (New York, 1832) describes this man as a *lusus nature*. "His skin was fair, his face partially freckled, and his hair quite red. He was about five feet ten inches high, was slender, but remarkably well made; his head had not undergone the flattening process. His father was a sailor who had deserted from an English ship. His name, Jack Ramsay, was tattooed on the son's arm. Poor Jack was fond of his father's countrymen, and had the decency to wear trousers whenever he came to the fort (Astoria). We therefore made a collection of old clothes for his use; sufficient to last him many years." —Ed.

FROM FORT CLATSOP TO MUSQUETOE CREEK

January 27, 1806–May 7, 1806

[Lewis] January 27, 1806

Goodrich has recovered from the Louis Veneri [*lues veneris*] which he contracted from an amorous contact with a Chinnook damsel. I cured him as I did Gibson last winter by the uce of murcury. I cannot learn that the Indians have any simples which are sovereign specifics in the cure of this disease; and indeed I doubt very much whether any of them have any means of effecting a perfect cure. Notwithstanding that this disorder dose exist among the Indians on the Columbia yet it is witnessed in but few individuals, at least the males who are always sufficiently exposed to the observations or inspection of the phisician.

[Lewis] February 2, 1806

One of the games of amusement and wrisk of the Indians of this neighbourhood like that of the Sosones consists in hiding in the hand some small article about the size of a bean; this they throw from one hand to the other with great dexterity accompanying their opperations with a particular song which seems to have been addapted to the game. When the individual who holds the peice has amused himself sufficiently by exchanging it from one hand to the other, he hold out his hands for his compettitors to guess which hand contains the peice. If they hit on the hand which contains the peice they win the wager, otherwise loose. The individual who holds the peice is a kind of banker and plays for a time being against all the others in the room. When he has lost all the property which he has to venture, or thinks proper at anytime, he transfers the peice to some other who then also becomes banker.

The natives here have also another game which consists in bowling some small round peices about the size of bacgammon men, between two small upright sticks placed a few inches asunder. But the principals of the game I have not learned, not understanding their language sufficiently to obtain an explanation.

[Lewis] February 7, 1806

This evening we had what I call an excellent supper. It consisted of a marrowbone, a piece and a brisket of boiled elk that had the appearance of a little fat on it. This for Fort Clatsop is living in high stile.

[Lewis] February 14, 1806

Capt. Clark completed a map of the country through which we have been passing from Fort Mandan to this place. In this map the Missouri, Jefferson's river, the S.E. branch of the Columbia, Kooskooske and Columbia from the entrance of the S.E. fork to the pacific ocean as well as a part of Flathead (Clarks) River and our tract [track] across the Rocky Mountains are laid down by celestial observation and survey. The rivers are also connected at their sources with other rivers agreeably to the information of the natives and the most probable conjecture arrising from their capacities and the relative positions of their respective entrances which last have with but few exceptions been established by celestial observation. We now discover that we have found the most practicable and navigable passage across the continent of North America. . . .

[Lewis] February 15, 1806

In this extensive tract of principally untimbered country so far as we have learnt the following natives reside (viz) the Sosone or Snake Indians, the Chopunnish, Sokulks, Cutssahnims, Chymnapums, Echelutes, Eneshuh & Chilluckkittequaws, all of whom enjoy the bennefit of that docile, generous and valuable anamal the horse, and all of them except the three last have immence numbers of them.

Their horses appear to be of an excellent race; they are lofty, elegantly formed, active and durable. In short many of them look like the fine English coarsers and would make a figure in any country. Some of those horses are pided [pied] with large spots of white irregularly scattered and intermixed with the black brown bey or some other dark colour, but much the larger portion are of an uniform colour with stars, snips and white feet, or in this rispect marked much like our best blooded horses in Virginia, which they resemble as well in fleetness and bottom as in form and colours. An eligant horse may be purchased of the natives in this country for a few beads or other paltry trinkets which in the U'States would not cost more than one or two dollars. . . . Among the Sosones of the upper part of the S.E. fork of the Columbia we saw several horses with Spanish brands on them which we supposed had been stolen from the inhabitants of Mexeco.

[Lewis] February 20, 1806

This forenoon we were visited by *Tah-cum* a principal chief of the Chinnooks and 25 men of his nation. We had never seen this cheif before. He is a good looking man of about 50 years of age reather larger in stature than most of his nation. As he came on a friendly visit we gave himself and party something to eat and plyed them plentifully with smoke. We gave this cheif a small medal with which he seemed much gratifyed. In the evening at sunset we desired them to depart as is our custom and closed our gates. We never suffer parties of such number to remain within the fort all night; for notwithstanding their apparent friendly disposition, their great averice and hope of plunder might induce them to be treacherous. At all events we determined always to be on our guard as much as the nature of our situation will permit us, and never place ourselves at the mercy of any savages. We well know, that the treachery of the aborigenes of America and the too great confidence of our countrymen in their sincerity and friendship, has caused the distruction of many hundreds of us.

[Lewis] February 22, 1806

We were visited today by two Clatsop women and two boys who brought a parsel of excellent hats made of cedar bark and ornamented with beargrass. Two of these hats had been made by measures which Capt. Clark and myself had given one of the women some time since with a request to make each of us a hat. They fit us very well, and are in the form we desired them.

[Lewis] March 15, 1806

We were visited this afternoon by *Delash-shelwilt,* a Chinnook chief his wife and six women of his nation which the Old Boud his wife had brought for market. This was the same party that had communicated the venereal to so many of our party in November last, and of which they have finally recovered. I therefore gave the men a particular charge with rispect to them which they promised me to observe.

[Lewis] March 19, 1806

The Killamucks, Clatsops, Chinnooks, Cathlahmahs and Wâc-ki-a-cums resemble each other as well in their persons and dress as in their habits and manners. . . . The most remarkable trait in their physiognomy is the peculiar flatness and width of forehead which they artificially obtain by compressing the head between two boards while in a state of infancy and from which it never afterwards perfectly recovers. This is a custom among all the nations we have met with west of the Rocky Mountains. I have observed the heads of many infants, after this singular bandage had been dismissed, or about the age of 10 or eleven months, that were not more than two inches thick about the upper edge of the forehead and reather thiner still higher. From the top of the head to the extremity of the nose is one streight line.

This is done in order to give a greater width to the forehead, which they much admire. This process seems to be continued longer with their female than their mail children, and neither appear to suffer any pain from the operation. It is from this peculiar form of the head that the nations east of the Rocky Mountains, call all the nations on this side, except the Aliohtans or Snake Indians, by the generic name of Flatheads. . . .

The dress of the women consists of a robe, tissue, and sometimes when the weather is uncommonly cold, a vest. . . . The garment which occupys the waist, and from thence as low as nearly to the knee before and the ham, behind, cannot properly be denominated a petticoat, in the common acceptation of that term; it is a tissue of white cedar bark, bruised or broken into small shreds, which are interwoven in the middle by means of several cords of the same materials, which serve as well for a girdle as to hold in place tire shreds of bark which form the tissue, and which shreds confined in the middle hang with their ends pendulous from the waist, the whole being of sufficient thickness when the female stands erect to conceal those parts usually covered from formiliar view. But when she stoops or places herself in many other attitudes, this battery of Venus is not altogether impervious to the inquisitive and penetrating eye of the amorite. . . .

I think the most disgusting sight I have ever beheld is these dirty naked wenches. The men of these nations partake of much more of the domestic drudgery than I had at first supposed. They collect and prepare all the fuel, make the fires, assist in cleansing and preparing the fish, and always cook for the strangers who visit them. They also build their houses, construct their canoes, and make all their wooden utensils. The peculiar provence of the woman seems to be to collect roots and manufacture various articles which are prepared of rushes, flags, cedarbark, bear grass or waytape. The management of the canoe for various purposes seems to be a duty common to both sexes, as also many other occupations which with most Indian nations devolves exclusively on the woman. Their feasts, of which they are very fond, are always prepared and served by the men.

[Lewis] March 30, 1806

The natives who inhabit this valley are larger and reather better made than those of the coast. Like those people they are fond of cold, hot, & vapor baths of which they make frequent uce both in sickness and in health and at all seasons of the year. They have also a very singular custom among them of baithing themselves all over with urine every morning.

We had a view of mount St. Helines and Mount Hood. The 1ˢᵗ is the most noble looking object of it's kind in nature. It's figure is a regular cone. Both these mountains are perfectly covered with snow; at least the parts of them which are visible.

As spring approached, Lewis and Clark became anxious to leave Fort Clatsop and its incessant rains behind to return home. But they faced a dilemma: if they waited too long for the salmon run up the Columbia to give them food, they might not descend the Missouri before winter again closed the river.

[Lewis] April 1, 1806

We were visited by several canoes of natives in the course of the day; most of whom were decending the river with their women and children. They informed us that they resided at the great rapids and that their relations at that place were much streighened at that place for want of food; that they had consumed their winter store of dryed fish and that those of the present season had not yet arrived. . . . They informed us that the nations above them were in the same situation & that they did not expect the salmon to arrive untill the full of the next moon which happens on the 20th of May. . . . This information gave us much uneasiness with rispect to our future means of subsistence. Above [the] falls or through the plains from thence to the Chopunnish [Nez Perce] there are no deer antelope nor elk on which we can depend for subsistence. Their horses are very poor most probably at this season, and if they have no fish their dogs must be in the same situation. Under these circumstances there seems to be but a gloomy prospect for subsistence on any terms.

We therefore took it into serious consideration what measures we were to pursue on this occasion; it was at once deemed inexpedient to wait the arrival of the salmon as that would detain us so large a portion of the season that it is probable we should not reach the United States before the ice would close the Missouri; or at all events would hazard our horses which we left in charge of the Chopunnish who informed us they intended passing the Rocky Mountains to the Missouri as early as the season would permit them which was we believe about the begining of May. Should these people leave their situation near Kooskooske [Clearwater] before our arrival we may probably find much difficulty in recovering our horses; without which there will be but little possibility of repassing the mountains. We are therefore determined to loose as little time as possible in geting to the Chopunnish village.

I purchased a canoe from an Indian today for which I gave him six fathoms of wampum beads. He seemed satisfyed with his bargain and departed in another canoe but shortly after returned and canceled the bargain, took his canoe and returned the beads. This is frequently the case in their method of traiding and is deemed fair by them.

[Lewis] April 11, 1806

We concluded to take our canoes first to the head of the rapids, hoping that by evening the rain would cease and afford us a fair afternoon to take our baggage over the portage. This portage is two thousand eight hundred yards along a narrow rough and slipery road. The duty of getting the canoes above the rapid was by mutual consent confided to my friend Capt. C. who took with him for that purpose all the party except Bratton who is yet so weak he is unable to work, three others who were lamed by various accedents, and one other to cook for the party. A few men were absolutely necessary at any rate to guard our baggage from the War-clel-lars who crowded about our camp in considerable numbers. These are the greatest theives and scoundrels we have met with.

By the evening Capt. C. took four of our canoes above the rapids tho' with much difficulty and labour. The canoes were much damaged by being driven against the rocks in dispite of every precaution which could betaken to prevent [i]t. . . . Many of the natives crouded about the bank of the river where the men were engaged in taking up the canoes. One of them had the insolence to cast stones down the bank at two of the men who happened to be a little detatched from the party at the time.

On the return of the party in the evening from the head of the rapids they met with many of the natives on the road, who seemed but illy disposed; two of these fellows met with John Sheilds who had delayed some time in purchasing a dog and was a considerable distance behind the party on their return with Capt. C. They attempted to take the dog from him and pushed him out of the road. He had nothing to defend himself with except a large knife which he drew with an intention of puting one or both of them to death before they could get themselves in readiness to use their arrows. But discovering his design they declined the combat and instantly fled through the woods.

Three of this same tribe of villains, the Wah-clel-lars, stole my dog this evening, and took him towards their village. I was shortly afterwards informed of this transaction by an Indian who spoke the Clatsop language and sent three men in pursuit of the theives with orders if they made the least resistance or difficulty in surrendering the dog to fire on them. They overtook these fellows or reather came within sight of them at the distance of about 2 miles. The Indians discovering the party in pursuit of them left the dog and fled. They also stole an ax from us, but scarcely had it in their possession before Thompson detected them and wrested it from them. We ordered the centinel to keep them out of camp, and informed them by signs that if they made any further attempts to steal our property or insulted our men we should put them to instant death. A cheif of the Clah-clel-lah tribe informed us that there were two very bad men among the Wah-clel-lahs who had been the principal actors in these seenes of outradge of which we complained, and that it was not the wish of the nation by any means to displease us. We told him that we hoped it might be the case, but we should certainly be as good as our words if they persisted in their insolence. I am convinced that no other consideration but our number at this moment protects us.[1]

[Lewis] April 19, 1806

There was great joy with the natives last night in consequence of the arrival of the salmon. One of those fish was caught; this was the harbinger of good news to them. They informed us that these fish would arrive in great quantities in the course of about 5 days. This fish was dressed and being divided into small peices was given to each child in the village. This custom is founded in a supersticious opinion that it will hasten the arrival of the salmon.

With much difficulty we obtained four other horses from the Indians today. We were obliged to dispence with two of our kettles, in order to acquire those. We have now only one small kettle to a mess of 8 men.

[Lewis] April 21, 1806

Notwithstanding all the precautions I had taken with rispect to the horses one of them had broken his cord of 5 strands of elkskin and had gone off spanseled. I sent several men in surch of the horse with orders to return at 10 a.m. with or without the horse being determined to remain no longer with these villains. They stole another tomahawk from us this morning. I surched many of them but could not find it. I ordered all the spare poles, paddles and the ballance of our canoes put on the fire as the morning was cold and also that not a particle should be left for the benefit of the Indians.

I detected a fellow in stealing an iron socket of a canoe pole and gave him several severe blows and made the men kick him out of camp. I now informed the Indians that I would shoot the first of them that attempted to steal an article from us that we were not affraid to fight them, that I had it in my power at that moment to kill them all and set fire to the houses, but it was not my wish to treat them with severity provided they would let my property alone. That I would take their horses if I could find out the persons who had stole the tommahawks, but that I had reather loose the property altogether than take the horse of an inosent person.

[Lewis] April 22, 1806

Charbono purchased a horse this evening. We obtained 4 dogs and as much wood as answered our purposes on moderate terms. We can only afford ourselves one fire, and are obliged to lie without shelter.

The nights are cold and days warm.

[Lewis] April 23, 1806

We passed five lodges of the same people [Wah-how-pum] who like those were waiting the arrival of the salmon. After we had arranged our camp we caused all the old and brave men to set arround and smoke with us. We had the violin played and some of the men danced; after which the natives entertained us with a dance after their method. This dance differed from any I have yet seen. They formed a circle and all sung as well the spectators as the dancers who performed within the circle. These placed their sholders together with their robes tightly drawn about them and danced in a line from side to side, several parties of from 4 to seven will be performing within the circle at the same time. The whole concluded with a premiscuous dance in which most of them sung and danced.

They brought several diseased persons to us for whom they requested some medical aid. One had his knee contracted by the rheumatism, another with a broken arm &c., to all of which we administered much to the gratification of those poor wretches. We gave them some eyewater which I beleive will render them more essential service than any other article in the medical way which we had it in our power to bestoe on them. *[Cap. C. splintered the arm of the man which hwas broke.]* Soar eyes seem to be a universal complaint amonge these people; I have no doubt but the fine sand of these plains and river (fishing on the waters too) contribute much to this disorder.

A little before sunset the Chymnahpos arrived. They were about 100 men and a few women; they joined the Wallahwollahs who were about the same number and formed a half circle arround our camp where they waited very patiently to see our party dance. The fiddle was played, and the men amused themselves with dancing about an hour. We then requested the Indians to dance which they very cheerfully complyed with. They continued their dance untill 10 at night. The whole assemblage of Indians, about 550 men, women and children sung and danced at the same time. Most of them stood in the same place and merely jumped up to the time of their music. Some of the men who were esteemed most brave entered the spase arrond which the main body were formed in solid column, and danced in a circular manner sidewise. At 10 p.m. the dance concluded and the natives retired. They were much gratifyed with seeing some of our party join them in their dance.

[Clark] April 29, 1806

Several [Indians] applyed to me to day for medical aide, one a broken arm another inward fevers and several with pains across their loins, and sore eyes. I administered as well as I could to all. In the evening a man brought his wife and a horse both up to me. The horse he gave me as a present and his wife who was verry unwell [with] the effects of violent coalds was placed before me. I did not think her case a bad one and gave such medesene as would keep her body open and raped her in flannel.

[Lewis] April 30, 1806

We exchanged one of our indifferent horses for a very good one with the Chopunnish man who has his family with him. This man has a daughter new arrived at the age of puberty, who being in a certain situation [mences] is not permitted to ascociate with the family but sleeps at a distance from her father's camp and when traveling follows at some distance behind. In this state I am informed that the female is not permitted to eat, nor to touch any article of a culinary nature or manly occupation.

[Lewis] May 1, 1806

Some time after we had encamped, three young men arrived from the Wallahwollah village bringing with them a steel trap belonging to one of our party which had been neglegently left behind. This is an act of integrity rarely witnessed among Indians. During our stay with them they several times found the knives of the men which had been carelessly lossed by them and returned them. I think we can justly affirm to the honor of these people that they are the most hospitable, honest, and sincere people that we have met within our voyage.

[Lewis] May 5, 1806

At the second lodge we passed an Indian man [who] gave Capt. C. a very eligant grey mare for which he requested a phial of eyewater which was accordingly given him. While we were encamped last fall at the entrance of the Chopunnish river Capt. C. gave an Indian man some volitile linniment to rub his knee and thye for a pain of which he complained. The fellow soon after recovered and has never ceased to extol the virtues of our medicines and the skill of my friend Capt. C. as a phisician. This occurrence added to the benefit which many of them experienced from the eyewater we gave them about the same time [and] has given them an exalted opinion of our medicine. My friend Capt. C. is their favorite phisician and has already received many applications.

In our present situation I think it pardonable to continue this deseption for they will not give us any provision without compensation in merchandize and our stock is now reduced to a mere handfull. We take care to give them no article which can possibly injure them. . . .

While at dinner an Indian fellow verry impertinently threw a poor half starved puppy nearly into my plait by way of derision for our eating dogs and laughed very heartily at his own impertinence. I was so provoked at his insolence that I caught the puppy and threw it with great violence at him and struck him in the breast and face, siezed my tomahawk and shewed him by signs if he repeated his insolence I would tommahawk him. The fellow withdrew apparently much mortifyed and I continued my repast on dog without further molestation.

[Lewis] May 7, 1806

The spurs of the Rocky Mountains which were in view from the high plain today were perfectly covered with snow. The Indians inform us that the snow is yet so deep on the mountains that we shall not be able to pass them untill the next full moon or about the first of June; others set the time at still a more distant period. This is unwelcom inteligence to men confined to a diet of horse-beef and roots, and who are as anxious as we are to return to the fat plains of the Missouri and thence to our native homes.

---

1. Doubtless the expedition was protected from greater insult by its size alone. A party of fifteen traders under Alexander Stuart and James Keith were driven back from the Cascades in 1813, and several wounded. —Ed.

VOLUME FIVE

From Musquetoe Creek
to St. Louis

May 8, 1806–September 26, 1806

*The party moved back into Nez Perce country in Idaho, just west of
the Bitterroots. The explorers were anxious to push further to the east, but
it would be a full month before they could begin to cross the formidable
mountains that had almost stopped the expedition the previous fall.*

[Lewis] May 10, 1806

At 4 in the afternoon we decended the hills to Commearp
Creek and arrived at the Village of Tunnachemootoolt, the cheif at
whos lodge we had left the flag last fall. . . . We collected the cheifs
and men of consideration [and] smoked with them and stated our
situation with rispect to provision. The cheif spoke to his people
and they produced us about 2 bushels of the quawmas roots dryed,
four cakes of the bread of cows and a dryed salmon trout. We

thanked them for this store of provision but informed them that our men not being accustomed to live on roots alone we feared it would make them sick, to obviate which we proposed exchangeing a [good] horse in reather low order for a young horse in tolerable order with a view to kill.

The hospitality of the cheif revolted at the eydea of an exchange. He told us that his young men had a great abundance of young horses and if we wished to eat them we should by [be] furnished with as many as we wanted. Accordingly they soon produced us two fat young horses, one of which we killed. The other we informed them we would pospone killing untill we had consumed the one already killed. This is a much greater act of hospitality than we have witnessed from any nation or tribe since we have passed the Rocky Mountains.

The village of the *Broken Arm* as I have heretofore termed it consists of one house only which is 150 feet in length built in the usual form of sticks matts and dry grass. It contains twenty four fires and about double that number of families.

The noise of their women pounding roots reminds me of a nail factory.

[Clark] May 11, 1806

In the evening a man was brought in a robe by four Indians and laid down near me. They informed me that this man was a chief of considerable note who has been in the situation I see him for 5 years. This man is incapable of moveing a single limb but lies like a corps in whatever position he is placed, yet he eats hartily, dejests his food perfectly, enjoys his understanding. His pulse are good, and has retained his flesh almost perfectly; in short were it not that he appears a little pale from having been so long in the shade, he might well be taken for a man in good health.

[Lewis] May 12, 1806

This morning a great number of Indians collected about us as usual. We took an early breakfast and Capt. C. began to administer eyewater to a croud of at least 50 applicants.

We are anxious to procure some guides to accompany us on the different tours we mean to take from Travellers Rest;' for this purpose we have turned our attention to the *Twisted Hair* who has several sons grown who are well acquainted as well as himself with the various roads in those mountains. We invited the old fellow to remove his family and live near us while we remained; he appeared gratified with this expression of our confidence and promised to do so.

Shot at a mark with the Indians. Struck the mark with 2 balls dist. 220 yds.

[Lewis] May 13, 1806

This morning Capt. C. as usual was busily engaged with his patients untill eleven Oclock. In the evening we tryed the speed of several of our horses. These horses are active strong and well formed. These people have immence numbers of them. 50, 60 or a hundred hed is not unusual for an individual to possess. The Chopunnish are in general stout, well formed, active men. They have high noses and many of them on the acqueline order with cheerfull and agreeable countenances their complexions are not remarkable. In common with other savage nations of America they extract their beards but the men do not uniformly extract the hair below. This is more particularly confined to the females. I observed several men among them whom I am convinced if they had shaved their beard instead of extracting it would have been as well supplyed in this particular as any of my countrymen.

They appear to be cheerfull but not gay; they are fond of gambling and of their amusements which consist principally in shooting their arrows at a bowling target made of willow bark, and in riding and exercising themselves on horseback, racing &c. They are expert marksmen and good riders. They do not appear to be so much devoted to baubles as most of the nations we have met with, but seem anxious always to obtain articles of utility, such as knives, axes, tommahawks, kettles blankets and mockersonalls [awls]. Blue beads however may form an exception to this remark; this article among all the nations of this country may be justly compared to goald or silver among civilized nations.

I observed a tippit woarn by *Hoha'stillpilp,*[2] which was formed of human scalps and ornamented with the thumbs and fingers of several men which he had slain in battle.

[Lewis] May 14, 1806

Collins killed two bear this morning and was sent with two others in quest of the meat; with which they returned in the evening. . . . We gave the Indians who were about 15 in number half the female bear, with the sholder head and neck of the other. This was a great treat to those poor wretches who scarcely taist meat once month. They immediately prepared a brisk fire of dry wood on which they threw a parsel of smooth stones from the river. When the fire had birnt down and heated the stones they placed them level and laid on a parsel of pine boughs. On these they laid the flesh of the bear in flitches, placing boughs between each course of meat and then covering it thickly with pine boughs. After this they poared on a small quantity of water and covered the who[l]e over with earth to the debth of four inches. In this situation they suffered it to remain about 3 hours when they took it out. I taisted of this meat and found it much more tender than that which we had roasted or boiled, but the strong flavor of the pine destroyed it for my pallate.

We have found our stonehorses [stallions] so troublesome that we indeavoured to exchange them with the Chopunnish for mears or geldings but they will not exchange altho we offer 2 for one. We came to a resolution to castrate them and began the operation this evening. One of the Indians present offered his services on this occasion. He cut them without tying the string of the stone as is usual, and assures us that they will do much better in that way. He takes care to scrape the string very clean and to seperate it from all the adhereing veigns before he cuts it. We shall have an opportunity of judging whether this is a method preferable to that commonly practiced as Drewyer has gelded two in the usual way.

The Indians after their feast took a pipe or two with us and retired to rest much pleased with their repast. These bear are tremendious animals to them; they esteem the act of killing a bear equally great with that of an enimy in the field of action.

[Lewis] May 16, 1806

Sahcargarweah geathered a quantity of the roots of a speceis of fennel which we found very agreeable food. The flavor of this root is not unlike annis seed, and they dispell the wind which the roots called cows and quawmash are apt to create, particularly the latter.

[Lewis] May 19, 1806

We amused ourselves about an hour this afternoon in looking at the men running their horses. Several of those horses would be thought fleet in the U. States.

[Lewis] May 24, 1806

The child [Sacagawea's son, Jean-Baptiste] was very wrestless last night. It's jaw and the back of it's neck are much more swolen than they were yesterday, tho' his fever has abated considerably. We gave it a doze of creem of tartar and applyed a fresh poltice of onions. William Bratton still continues very unwell; he eats heartily digests his food well, and has recovered his flesh almost perfectly yet is so weak in the loins that he is scarcely able to walk, nor can he set upwright but with the greatest pain. We have tried every remidy which our engnuity could devise, or with which our stock of medicines furnished us, without effect.

John Sheilds observed that he had seen men in a similar situation restored by violent sweats. Bratton requested that be might be sweated in the manner proposed by Sheilds to which we consented. Sheilds sunk a circular hole of 3 feet diamiter and four feet deep in the earth. He kindled a large fire in the hole and heated well, after which the fire was taken out a seat placed in the center of the hole for the patient with a board at bottom for his feet to rest on; some hoops of willow poles were bent in an arch crossing each other over the hole, on these several blankets were thrown forming a secure and thick orning of about 3 feet high. The patient being striped naked was seated under this orning in the hole and the blankets well secured on every side.

The patient was furnished with a vessell of water which he sprinkles on the bottom and sides of the hole and by that means creates as much steam or vapor as he could possibly bear. In this situation he was kept about 20 minutes after which he was taken out and suddonly plunged in cold water twise and was then immediately returned to the sweat hole where he was continued three quarters of an hour longer then taken out covered up in several blankets and suffered to cool gradually. During the time of his being in the sweat hole, he drank copious draughts of a strong tea of horse mint. Sheilds says that he had previously seen the tea of Sinneca snake root used in stead of the mint which was now employed for the want of the other which is not to be found in this country.

This experiment was made yesterday. Bratton feels himself much better and is walking about today and says he is nearly free from pain.

At 11 A.M. a canoe arrived with 3 of the natives, one of them the sick man of whom I have before made mention as having lost the

power of his limbs. He is a cheif of considerable note among them
and they seem extreemly anxious for his recovery. As he complains of
no pain in any particular part we conceive it cannot be the rheumatism, nor do we suppose that it can be a parelitic attack or his limbs
would have been more deminished. We have supposed that it was
some disorder which owed its origine to a diet of particular roots perhaps and such as we have never before witnessed.

While at the village of the *Broken Arm* we had recommended a
diet of fish or flesh for this man and the cold bath every morning. We
had also given him a few dozes of creem of tarter and flour of sulpher
to be repeated every 3rd day. This poor wretch thinks that he feels
himself somewhat better but to me there appears to be no visible
alteration. We are at a loss what to do for this unfortunate man. We
gave him a few drops of laudanum and a little portable soup.

[Lewis] May 27, 1806

Hohastillpilp told us that most of the horses we saw runing at
large in this neighbourhood belonged to himself and his people,
and whenever we were in want of meat he requested that we
would kill any of them we wished. This is a piece of liberallity
which would do honour to such as boast of civilization. Indeed I
doubt whether there are not a great number of our countrymen
who would see us fast many days before their compassion would
excite them to a similar act of liberallity.

Charbono's son is much better today, tho' the swelling on the
side of his neck I beleive will terminate in an ugly imposthume a
little below the ear.

The Indians were so anxious that the sick cheif should be sweated
under our inspection that they requested we would make a second
attempt today. Accordingly the hole was somewhat enlarged and his
father, a very good looking old man, went into the hole with him and
sustained him in a proper position during the operation; we could

not make him sweat as copiously as we wished. After the operation he complained of considerable pain, we gave him 30 drops of laudanum which soon composed him and he rested very well. This is at least a strong mark of parental affection. They all appear extreemly attentive to this sick man nor do they appear to relax in their asciduity towards him notwithstanding he has been sick and helpless upwards of three years.

[Lewis] May 28, 1806

The sick cheif was much better this morning. He can use his hands and arms and seems much pleased with the prospect of recovering. He says he feels much better than he has for a great number of months. I sincerely wish these sweats may restore him. We have consented that he should still remain with us and repeat these sweats.

The child is also better, he is free of fever, the imposthume is not so large but seems to be advancing to maturity.

[Lewis] May 29, 1806

Our horses maney of them have become so wild that we cannot take them without the assistance of the Indians who are extreemly dextrous in throwing a rope and takeing them with a noose about the neck. As we frequently want the use of our horses when we cannot get the use of the Indians to take them, we had a strong pound formed to day in order to take them at pleasure.

[Lewis] June 2, 1806

My sick horse being much reduced and apearing to be in such an agony of pain that there was no hope of his recovery. I ordered him shot this evening. The other horses which we casterated are all nearly recovered, and I have no hesitation in declaring my beleif that the Indian method of gelding is prefereable to that practiced by ourselves.

[Lewis] June 8, 1806

The sick cheif is fast on the recovery, he can bear his weight on his legs, and has acquired a considerable portion of strength. The child is nearly well. Bratton has so far recovered that we cannot well consider him an invalid any longer. He has had a tedious illness which he boar with much fortitude and firmness.

Several foot races were run this evening between the Indians and our men. The Indians are very active; one of them proved as fleet as Drewyer and R. Fields, our swiftest runners. When the racing was over the men divided themselves into two parties and played prison base, by way of exercise which we wish the men to take previously to entering the mountain. In short those who are not hunters have had so little to do that they are geting reather lazy and slouthfull. After dark we had the violin played and danced for the amusement of ourselves and the Indians.

One of the Indians informed us that we could not pass the mountains untill the full of the next moon or about the first of July, that if we attempted it sooner our horses would be at least three days travel without food on the top of the mountain. This information is disagreeable inasmuch as it causes some doubt as to the time at which it will be most proper for us to set out. However as we have no time to loose we will wrisk the chances and set out as early as the Indians generally think it practicable or the middle of this month.

[Lewis] June 9, 1806

We eat the last of our meat yesterday evening and have lived on roots today. Our party seem much elated with the idea of moving on towards their friends and country. They all seem allirt in their movements today. They have everything in readiness for a move, and notwithstanding the want of provision have been amusing themselves very merrily today in running foot races, pitching quites [qoits], prison basse &etc.

[Lewis] June 14, 1806

We have now been detained near five weeks in consequence of the snows; a serious loss of time at this delightfull season for traveling. I am still apprehensive that the snow and the want of food for our horses will prove a serious embarrassment to us as at least four days journey of our rout in these mountains lies over hights and along a ledge of mountains never intirely destitute of snow.

Every body seems anxious to be in motion, convinced that we have not now any time to delay if the calculation is to reach the United States this season; this I am determined to accomplish if within the compass of human power.

[Clark] June 14, 1806

Now I shudder with the expectation with [of] great dificuelties in passing those mountains, from the debth of snow and the want of grass sufficient to subsist our horses, as about 4 days we shall be on the top of the mountain which we have every reason to beleive is covered with snow the greater part of the year.

[Lewis] June 17, 1806

We proceeded down hungry creek about seven miles passing it twice. We found it difficult and dangerous to pass the creek in consequence of its debth and rapidity; we avoided two other passes of the creek by ascending a very steep rocky and difficult hill . . . we ascended about 3 miles when we found ourselves invelloped in snow from 12 to 15 feet deep even on the south sides of the hills with the fairest exposure to the sun.

Here was winter with all its rigors. The air was cold, my hands and feet were benumbed. We knew that it would require five days to reach the fish wears at the entrance of Colt Creek, provided we were so fortunate as to be enabled to follow the proper ridges of the mountains to lead us to that place. Drewyer, our principal dependence as a woodman and guide, was entirely doubtfull. Short of that point we could not hope for any food for our horses not even under-wood itself as the whole was covered many feet deep in snow. If we proceeded and should get bewildered in these mountains the certainty was that we should loose all our horses and consequently our baggage, instruments, perhaps our papers and thus eminently wrisk the loss of the discoveries which we had already made if we should be so fortunate as to escape with life.

The snow boar our horses very well and the travelling was therefore infinitely better than the obstruction of rocks and fallen timber which we met with in our passage over last fall when the snow lay on this part of the ridge in detached spots only. Under these circumstances we conceived it madness in this stage of the expedition to proceed without a guide who could certainly conduct us to the fish wears on the Kooskooske [*Travellers (Creek) Rest*],[3] as our horses could not possibly sustain a journey of more than five days without food.

We therefore came to the resolution to return with our horses while they were yet strong and in good order and indevour to keep them so untill we could procure an indian to conduct us over the snowey mountains. . . . We left our instruments papers &c. beleiving them safer here than to wrisk them on horseback over the roads and creeks which we had passed. . . . We returned by the rout we had come to Hungry Creek, which we ascended about 2 miles and encamped. We had here more grass for our horses than the proceeding evening, yet it was but scant. The party were a good deel dejected tho' not as much so as I had apprehended they would have been.

This is the first time since we have been on this long tour that we have ever been compelled to retreat or make a retrograde march.

Retreating to the quawmash flats, the captains sent Drouillard and Shannon to hire guides from the Nez Perce at a high price: two rifles. On June 24, they began their second attempt to cross the Bitterroots.

[Lewis] June 25, 1806

Last evening the Indians entertained us with seting the fir trees on fire. They have a great number of dry lims near their bodies which when set on fire creates a very suddon and immence blaze from bottom to top of those tall trees. They are a beatifull object in this situation at night. This exhibition reminded me of a display of fireworks. The natives told us that their object in seting those trees on fire was to bring fair weather for our journey.

[Lewis] June 27, 1806

The road still continued on the heights of the same dividing ridge on which we had traveled yesterday for nine miles or to our encampment of (*the 17ᵗʰ*) of September last. . . . From this place we had an extensive view of these stupendous mountains principally covered with snow like that on which we stood; we were entirely surrounded by those mountains from which to one unacquainted with them it would have seemed impossible ever to have escaped; in short without the asistance of our guides I doubt much whether we who had once passed them could find our way to Travellers Rest in their present situation for the marked trees on which we had placed considerable reliance are much fewer and more difficult to find than we had apprehended. These fellows are most admireable pilots; we find the road wherever the snow has disappeared though it be only for a few hundred paces.

[Lewis] June 29, 1806

After dinner we continued our march seven miles further to the warm spring. . . . The prinsipal spring is about the temperature of the warmest baths used at the hot springs in Virginia. In this bath which had been prepared by the Indians by stoping the run with stone and gravel. I bathed and remained in 19 minutes. It was with dificulty I could remain thus long as it caused a profuse sweat. . . .

Both the men and Indians amused themselves with the use of a bath this evening. I observed that the Indians after remaining in the hot bath as long as they could bear it ran and plunged themselves into the creek the water of which is now as cold as ice can make it. After remaining here a few minutes they returned again to the warm bath, repeating this transision several times but always ending with the warm bath.[4]

[Lewis] June 30, 1806

In decending the creek this morning on the steep side of a high hill my horse sliped with both his hinder feet out of the road and fell. I also fell off backwards and slid near 40 feet down the hill before I could stop myself such was the steepness of the declivity; the horse was near falling on me in the first instance but fortunately recovers and we both escaped unhirt.

The party arrived at Travellers Rest on the evening of June 30. They then put into place the plan they had devised back at Fort Clatsop.

[Lewis] July 1, 1806

From this place I determined to go with a small party by the most direct rout to the falls of the Missouri, there to leave Thompson McNeal and Goodrich to prepare carriages and geer for the purpose of transporting the canoes and baggage over the portage, and myself and six volunteers to ascend Maria's River with a view to explore the country and ascertain whether any branch of that river lies as far north as lat. 50 and again return and join the party who are to decend the Missour, at the entrance of Maria's River. I now called for the volunteers to accompany me on this rout. Many turned out, from whom I scelected Drewyer the two Feildes, Werner, Frazier and Ser. Gass.

The other part of the men are to proceed with Capt. Clark to the head of Jefferson's River where we deposited sundry articles and left our canoes. From hence Sgt. Ordway with a party of men are to decend the river with the canoes; Capt. C. with the remaining ten including Charbono and York will proceed to the three forks of the Missouri.

Here he will build a canoe and decend the Yellowstone River with Charbono, the Indian woman, his servant York and five others to the Missouri where should he arrive first he will wait my arrival.

Sergt. Pryor with two other men are to proceed with the horses by land to the Mandans and thence to the British posts on the Assiniboin with a letter to Mr. Heney who we wish to engage to prevail on the Sioux Chiefs to join us on the Missouri, and accompany them with us to the seat of the general government.

LEWIS'S SHORT-CUT TO THE MISSOURI, AND EXPLORATION OF MARIA'S RIVER

Lewis's Journal, July 3–August 12, 1806

[Lewis] July 3, 1806

All arrangements being now compleated for carrying into effect the several scheemes we had planed for execution on our return, we saddled our horses and set out. I took leave of my worthy friend and companion Capt. Clark and the party that accompanyed him. I could not avoid feeling much concern on this occasion although I hoped this separation was only momentary.

Lewis and his group of men proceeded up today's Big Blackfoot River (the setting of Norman Maclean's A River Runs Through It*)* *and across the Dearborn and Sun (then Medicine) valleys before finally encountering the Missouri.*

[Lewis] July 11, 1806

The morning was fair, and the plains looked beatifull, the grass much improved by the late rain. The air was pleasant and a vast assemblage of little birds which crowd to the groves on the river sung most enchantingly.

We set out early . . . through a level beautifull and extensive high plain covered with immence hirds of buffaloes. It is now the season at which the buffaloe begin to coppelate and the bulls keep a tremendious roaring. We could hear them for many miles and there are such numbers of them that there is one continual roar. Our horses had not been acquainted with the buffaloe they appeared much allarmed at their appearance and bellowing. When I arrived in sight of the White-bear Islands the Missouri bottoms on both sides of the river were crouded with buffaloe. I sincerely beleif that there were not less than 10 thousand buffaloe within a circle of 2 miles arround that place.

[Lewis] July 15, 1806

A little before dark McNeal returned with his musquet broken off at the breach, and informed me that on his arrival at willow run [on the portage] he had approached a white bear within ten feet without discovering him the bear being in the thick brush. The horse took the allarm and turning short threw him immediately under the bear; this animal raised himself on his hinder feet for battle, and gave him time to recover from his fall which he did in an instant and with his clubbed musquet he struck the bear over the head and cut him with the guard of the gun and broke off the breech.

The bear stunned with the stroke fell to the ground and began to scratch his head with his feet. This gave McNeal time to climb a willow tree which was near at hand and thus fortunately made his escape. The bear waited at the foot of the tree untill late in the evening before he left him when McNeal ventured down and caught his horse which had by this time strayed off to the distance of 2 ms. and returned to camp.

These bear are a most tremenduous animal. It seems that the hand of providence has been most wonderfully in our favor with rispect to them, or some of us would long since have fallen a sacrifice to their farosity.

There seems to be a sertain fatality attatched to the neighbourhood of these falls, for there is always a chapter of accedents prepared for us during our residence at them. The musquetoes continue to infest us in such manner that we can scarcely exist. For my own part I am confined by them to my bier at least 3/4ths of my time. My dog even howls with the torture he experiences from them. They are almost insupportable, they are so numerous that we frequently get them in our throats as we breath.

Arriving at the Maria's River, Lewis turned north to explore its watershed. The river eventually forked at Cut Bank Creek and the Two-Medicine River. They were deep in Blackfeet country but thus far had avoided any encounters with the much-feared tribe.

[Lewis] July 26, 1806

After dinner I continued my rout down the river. . . . Drewyer passed the river and kept down the vally of the river. . . . I had scarcely ascended the hills before I discovered to my left at the distance of a mile an assembleage of about 30 horses. I halted and used my spye glass by the help of which I discovered several Indians on the top of an eminence just above them who appeared to be looking down towards the river, I presumed at Drewyer. About half the horses were saddled.

This was a very unpleasant sight. However I resolved to make the best of our situation and to approach them in a friendly manner. I directed J. Fields to display the flag which I had brought for that purpose and advanced slowly toward them. About this time they discovered us and appeared to run about in a very confused manner as if much allarmed. Their attention had been previously so fixed on Drewyer that they did not discover us untill we had began to advance upon them. Some of them decended the hill on which they were and drove their horses within shot of its summit and again returned to the hight as if to wate our arrival or to defend themselves.

I calculated on their number being nearly or quite equal to that of their horses, that our runing would invite pursuit as it would convince them that we were their enimies, and our horses were so indifferent that we could not hope to make our escape by flight. Added to this Drewyer was separated from us, and I feared that his not being apprized of the Indians in the event of our attempting to escape he would most probably fall a sacrefice.

Under these considerations I still advanced towards them. When we had arrived within a quarter of a mile of them, one of them mounted his horse and rode full speed towards us, which when I discovered I halted and alighted from my horse. He came within a hundred paces halted, looked at us and turned his horse about and returned as briskly to his party as he had advanced. While he halted near us I held out my hand and becconed to him to approach but he paid no attention to my overtures. On his return to his party they all decended the hill and mounted their horses and advanced towards us leaving their horses behind them. We also advanced to meet them. I counted eight of them but still supposed that there were others concealed as there were several other horses saddled.

I told the two men with me that I apprehended that these were the Minnetares of Fort de Prarie[5] and from their known character I expected that we were to have some difficulty with them; that if they thought themselves sufficiently strong I was convinced they would attempt to rob us in which case be their numbers what they would I should resist to the last extremity prefering death to that of being deprived of my papers, instruments and gun and desired that they would form the same resolution and be allert and on their guard.

When we arrived within a hundred yards of each other the Indians except one halted. I directed the two men with me to do the same and advanced singly to meet the Indian with whom I shook hands and passed on to those in his rear, as he did also to the two men in my rear. We now all assembled and alighted from our horses. The Indians soon asked to smoke with us, but I told them that the man whom they had seen pass down the river[6] had my pipe and we could not smoke untill he joined us.

I requested as they had seen which way he went that they would one of them go with one of my men in surch of him. This they readily concented to and a young man set out with R. Fields in surch of Drewyer. I now asked them by signs if they were the Minnetares of the north which they answered in the affermative. I asked if there was any cheif among them and they pointed out 3. I did not believe them. However I thought it best to please them and gave to one a medal, to a second a flag and to the third a handkerchief, with which they apeared well satisfyed. They appeared much agitated with our first interview from which they had scarcely yet recovered. In fact I beleive they were more allarmed at this accedental interview than we were. From no more of them appearing I now concluded they were only eight in number and became much better satisfyed with our situation as I was convinced that we could mannage that number should they attempt any hostile measures. As it was growing late in the evening I proposed that we should remove to the nearest part of the river and encamp together. . . .

The Indians formed a large semicircular camp of dressed buffaloe skins and invited us to partake of their shelter which Drewyer and myself accepted, and the Fieldses lay near the fire in front of the shelter. With the assistance of Drewyer I had much conversation with these people in the course of the evening learned from them that they were a part of a large band which lay encamped at present near the foot of the rocky mountains on the main branch of Maria's River one ½ days march from our present encampment; that there was a white man with their band; that there was another large band of their nation hunting buffaloe near the broken mountains and were on there way to the mouth of Maria's River where they would probably be in the course of a few days.

I took the first watch tonight and set up untill half after eleven; the Indians by this time were all asleep. I roused up R. Fields and laid down myself. I directed Fields to watch the movements of the Indians and if any of them left the camp to awake us all as I apprehended they would attampt to steal our horses. This being done I feel into a profound sleep and did not wake untill the noise of the men and Indians awoke me a little after light in the morning.

[Lewis] July 27, 1806

This morning at daylight the Indians got up and crouded around the fire. J. Fields who was on post had carelessly laid his gun down behind him near where his brother was sleeping. One of the Indians the fellow to whom I had given the medal last evening sliped behind him and took his gun and that of his brother unperceived by him. At the same instant two others advanced and seized the guns of Drewyer and myself.

J. Fields seeing this turned about to look for his gun and saw the fellow just runing off with her and his brother's. He called to his brother who instantly jumped up and pursued the Indian with him whom they overtook at the distance of 50 or 60 paces from the camp seized their guns and rested them from him and R. Fields as he seized his gun stabed the Indian to the heart with his knife. The fellow ran about 15 steps and fell dead; of this I did not know untill afterwards.[7] Having recovered their guns they ran back instantly to the camp.

Drewyer who was awake saw the Indian take hold of his gun and instantly jumped up and seized her and rested her from him but the Indian still retained his pouch. His jumping up and crying damn you let go my gun awakened me.

I jumped up and asked what was the matter which I quickly learned when I saw Drewyer in a scuffle with the Indian for his gun. I reached to seize my gun but found her gone. I then drew a pistol from my holster and terning myself about saw the Indian making off with my gun. I ran at him with my pistol and bid him lay down my gun which he was in the act of doing when the Fieldses returned and drew up their guns to shoot him which I forbid as he did not appear to be about to make any resistance or commit any offensive act.

He droped the gun and walked slowly off. I picked her up instantly. Drewyer having about this time recovered his gun and pouch asked me if he might not kill the fellow which I also forbid as the Indian did not appear to wish to kill us. As soon as they found us all in possession of our arms they ran and endeavored to drive off all the horses. I now hollowed to the men and told them to fire on them if they attempted to drive off our horses.

They accordingly pursued the main party who were driving the horses up the river and I pursued the man who had taken my gun who with another was driving off a part of the horses which were to the left of the camp. I pursued them so closely that they could not take twelve of their own horses but continued to drive one of mine with some others. At the distance of three hundred paces they entered one of those steep nitches in the bluff with the horses before them. Being nearly out of breath I could pursue no further.

I called to them as I had done several times before that I would shoot them if they did not give me my horse and raised my gun. One of them jumped behind a rock and spoke to the other who turned arround and stoped at the distance of 30 steps from me and I shot him through the belly. He fell to his knees and on his wright elbow from which position he partly raised himself up and fired at me, and turning himself about crawled in behind a rock which was a few feet from him. He overshot me; being bearheaded I felt the wind of his bullet very distinctly. Not having my shot pouch I could not reload my peice, and as there were two of them behind good shelters from me I did not think it prudent to rush on them with my pistol which had I discharged. I had not the means of reloading untill I reached camp. I therefore returned leasurely towards camp.

On my way I met with Drewyer who having heared the report of the guns had returned in surch of me and left the Fieldes to pursue the Indians. I desired him to haisten to the camp with me and assist in catching as many of the Indian horses as were necessary and to call to the Fieldses if he could make them hear to come back that we still had a sufficient number of horses. This he did but they were too far to hear him. We reached the camp and began to catch the horses and saddle them and put on the packs. The reason I had not my pouch with me was that I had not time to return about 50 yards to camp after geting my gun before I was obliged to pursue the Indians or suffer them to collect and drive off all the horses.

We had caught and saddled the horses and began to arrange the packs when the Fieldses returned with four of our horses. We left one of our horses and took four of the best of those of the Indians. While the men were preparing the horses I put four sheilds and two bows and quivers of arrows which had been left on the fire, with sundry other articles. They left all their baggage at our mercy.

They had but 2 guns and one of them they left. The others were armed with bows and arrows and eyedaggs.[8] The gun we took with us. I also retook the flagg but left the medal about the neck of the dead man that they might be informed who we were.

We took some of their buffaloe meat and set out ascending the bluffs by the same rout we had decended last evening leaving the ballance of nine of their horses which we did not want. The Fieldses told me that three of the Indians whom they pursued swam the river, one of them on my horse. And that two others ascended the hill and escaped from them with a part of their horses. Two I had pursued into the nitch; one lay dead near the camp and the eighth we could not account for but suppose that he ran off early in the contest.

My design was to hasten to the entrance of Maria's River as quick as possible in the hope of meeting with the canoes and party at that place having no doubt but that they [the Indians] would pursue us with a large party . . . no time was therefore to be lost and we pushed our horses as hard as they would bear. . . . After refreshing ourselves we again set out by moonlight and traveled leasurely, heavy thunderclouds lowered arround us on every quarter but that from which the moon gave us light.

We continued to pass immence herds of buffaloe all night as we had done in the latter part of the day. We traveled untill 2 Ock in the morning having come by my estimate after dark about 20 m. We now turned out our horses and laid ourselves down to rest in the plain very much fatiegued as may be readily conceived. My Indian horse carried me very well in short much better than my own would have done and leaves me with but little reason to complain of the robery.

[Lewis] July 28, 1806

I slept sound but fortunately awoke as day appeared. I awaked the men and directed the horses to be saddled. I was so soar from my ride yesterday that I could scarcely stand, and the men complained of being in a similar situation. . . . I told them that we owed much to the safety of our friends and that we must wrisk our lives on this occasion, that I should proceed immediately to the point and if the party had not arrived that I would raft the Missouri a small distance above, hide our baggage and march on foot up the river through the timber untill I met the canoes or joined them at the falls. I now told them that it was my determination that if we were attacked in the plains on our way to the point that the bridles of the horses should be tied together and we would stand and defend them, or sell our lives as dear as we could.

We had proceeded about 12 miles on an east course when we found ourselves near the Missouri; we heard a report which we took to be that of a gun but were not certain; still continuing down the N.E. bank of the Missouri about 8 miles further, being then within five miles of the grog spring" we heared the report of several rifles very distinctly on the river to our right. We quickly repaired to this joyfull sound and on arriving at the bank of the river had the unspeakable satisfaction to see our canoes coming down.

After reuniting his party with those of Sergeant Ordway and later Sergeants Gass and Willard, Lewis proceeded down the Missouri to the mouth of the Yellowstone and his intended rendezvous with Clark. But, having waited with no game nearby, Clark had meanwhile proceeded further downstream.

[Lewis] August 11, 1806

Just opposite to the birnt hills there happened to be a herd of elk on a thick willow bar, and finding that my observation was lost for the present I determined to land and kill some of them. Accordingly we put too and I went out with Cruzatte only. We fired on the elk. I killed one and he wounded another. We reloaded our guns and took different routs through the thick willows in pursuit of the elk. I was in the act of firing on the elk a second time when a ball struck my left thye about an inch below my hip joint, missing the bone it passed through the left thye and cut the thickness of the bullet across the hinder part of the right thye; the stroke was very severe.

I instantly supposed that Cruzatte had shot me in mistake for an elk as I was dressed in brown leather and he cannot see very well. Under this impression I called out to him damn you, you have shot me, and looked towards the place from whence the ball had come. Seeing nothing I called Cruzatte several times as loud as I could but received no answer. I was now preswaded that it was an Indian that had shot me as the report of the gun did not appear to be more than 40 paces from me and Cruzatte appeared to be out of hearing of me.

In this situation not knowing how many Indians there might be concealed in the bushes I thought best to make good my retreat to the perogue, calling out as I ran for the first hundred paces as loud as I could to Cruzatte to retreat that there were Indians, hoping to allarm him in time to make his escape also. I still retained the charge in my gun which I was about to discharge at the moment the ball struck me.

When I arrived in sight of the perogue I called the men to their arms to which they flew in an instant. I told them that I was wounded but I hoped not mortally, by an Indian I beleived and directed them to follow me that I would return & give them battle and releive Cruzatte if possible, who I feared had fallen into their hands. The men followed me as they were bid and I returned about a hundred paces when my wounds became so painfull and my thye so stiff that I could scarcely get on. In short I was compelled to halt and ordered the men to proceed and if they found themselves over-powered by numbers to retreat in order keeping up a fire.

I now got back to the perogue as well as I could and prepared my self with a pistol my rifle and air-gun being determined as a retreat was impracticable to sell my life as deerly as possible. In this state of anxiety and suspense I remained about 20 minutes when the party returned with Cruzatte and reported that there were no Indians nor the appearance of any.

Cruzatte seemed much allarmed and declared if he had shot me it was not his intention, that he had shot an elk in the willows after he left or separated from me. I asked him whether he did not hear me when I called to him so frequently which he absolutely denied. I do not beleive that the fellow did it intentionally but after finding that he had shot me was anxious to conceal his knowledge of having done so. The ball had lodged in my breeches which I knew to be the ball of the short rifles such as that he had, and there being no person out with me but him and no Indians that we could discover I have no doubt in my own mind of his having shot me.

With the assistance of Sergt. Gass I took off my cloaths and dressed my wounds myself as well as I could, introducing tents of patent lint into the ball holes. The wounds blead considerably but I was hapy to find that it had touched neither bone nor artery. As it was painfull to me to be removed I slept on board the perogue. The pain I experienced excited a high fever and I had a very uncomfortable night.

[Lewis] August 12, 1806

Being anxious to overtake Capt. Clark who from the appearance of his camps could be at no great distance before me, we set out early and proceeded with all possible expedition at 8 a.m. The bowsman informed me that there was a canoe and a camp he beleived of white men on the N.E. shore. I directed the perogue and canoes to come too at this place and found it to be the camp of two hunters from the Illinois by name Joseph Dickson and Forest Hancock.[10] These men informed me that Capt. C. had passed them about noon the day before. they also informed me that they had left the Illinois in the summer [of] 1804 since which time they had been ascended the Missouri, hunting and traping beaver; that they had been robed by the Indians and the former wounded last winter by the Tetons of the birnt woods; that they had hitherto been unsuccessful in their voyage having as yet caught but little beaver, but were still determined to proceed.

I gave them a short description of the Missouri, a list of distances to the most conspicuous streams and remarkable places on the river above and pointed out to them the places where the beaver most abounded. I also gave them a file and a couple of pounds of powder with some lead. These were articles which they assured me they were in great want of.

At 1 p.m. I overtook Capt. Clark and party and had the pleasure of finding them all well. As wrighting in my present situation is extreemly painfull to me I shall desist untill I recover and leave to my friend Capt. C. the continuation of our journal.

However I must notice a singular cherry which is found on the Missouri in the bottom lands about the beaver bends and some little distance below the white earth river. This production is not very abundant even in the small tract of country to which it seems to be confined."

Clark's Exploration of
the Yellowstone

Back on July 3, Clark had left Lewis at Traveller's Rest and headed south on the Bitterroot River with Sergeants Ordway and Pryor, seventeen soldiers, York, Toussaint Charbonneau, and Sacagawea and her son, Jean-Baptiste.

[Clark] July 3, 1806

Musquetors very troublesome. One man Jo. Potts very unwell this evening owing to rideing a hard trotting horse. Give him a pill of opiom which soon releved him.

[Clark] July 4, 1806

This being the day of the Decleration of Independence of the United States and a day commonly scelebrated by my country I had every disposition to selebrate this day and therefore halted early and partook of a sumptious dinner of a fat saddle of venison and mush of cows (roots).

[Clark] July 6, 1806

[We] entered an extensive open leavel plain in which the Indian trail scattered in such a manner that we could not pursue it. The Indian woman, wife to Shabono, informed me that she had been in this plain frequently and knew it well. That the creek which we decended was a branch of Wisdom River and when we assended the higher part of the plain we would discover a gap in the mountains in our direction to the canoes, and when we arived at that gap we would see a high point of a mountain covered with snow in our direction to the canoes. We proceeded on and crossd a large creek from the right which heads in a snow mountain and Fish Creek over which there was a road thro' a gap.[12] . . . We assended a small rise and beheld an open beutifull leavel vally or plain of about 20 (15) miles wide and near 60 (30) long, extending N. & S. in every direction around which I could see high points of mountains covered with snow. . . . The squar pointed to the gap through which she said we must pass.[13]

[Clark] July 9, 1806

The squar brought me a plant the root of which the nativs eat. This root resembles a carrot in form and size and something of its colour, being of a pailer yellow than that of our carrot, the stem and leaf is much like the common carrot, and the taste not unlike. It is a native of moist land.[14]

[Clark] July 13, 1806

Encamped on the bank of Gallitines River which is a butifiill navigable strearm.[15] Saw a large gange of elk in the plains and Deer in the river bottoms. . . . The country in the forks between Gallitins &

Madisens rivers is a butifull leavel plain covered with low grass. On the lower or N.E. side of Gallitins River the country rises gradually to the foot of a mountain which runs nearly parrelal. . . . I observe several leading roads which appear to pass to a gap of the mountain in a E.N.E. direction about 18 or 20 miles distant. The Indian woman who has been of great service to me as a pilot through this country recommends a gap in the mountain more south which I shall cross.[16]

[Clark] July 14, 1806

Here the squar informed me that there was a large road passing through the upper part of this low plain from Madicins River through the gap which I was stearing my course to. . . . I saw elk, deer & antelopes, and great deel of old signs of buffalow. Their roads is in every direction. The Indian woman informs me that a fiew years ago buffalow was very plenty in those plains & vallies quite as high as the head of Jeffersons River, but fiew of them ever come into those vallys of late years owing to the Shoshones who are fearfull of passing into the plains west of the mountains and subsist on what game they can catch in the mountains principally and the fish which they take in the E. fork of Lewis's River.

After dinner we proceeded on a little to the south of east through an open leavel plain to the three forks of the E. branch of Gallitines River at about 12 miles. Crossed the most southerly of those forks and struck an old buffalow road (*the one our Indn woman meant*) which I kept continuing nearly the same course up the middle fork crossed it and camped on a small branch of the middle fork on the N.E. side at the commencement of the gap of the mountain.

[Clark] July 15, 1806

At 8 a.m. set out and proceeded up the branch to the head thence over a low gap in the mountain thence across the heads of the N.E.

branch of the (*i.e., the easterly*) fork of Gallitins River which we camped near last night passing over a low dividing ridge to the head of a water course which runs into the Rochejhone [Yellowstone], prosueing an old buffalow road which enlargenes by one which joins it from the most eas'terly (*northerly*) branch of the East fork of Gale-tine R. proceeding down the branch a little to the N. of east keeping on the north side of the branch to the river *Rochejhone* at which place I arrived at 2 p.m.[17]

[Clark] *July 21, 1806*

This morning I was informed that half of our horses were absent.... I am apprehensive that the Indians have stolen our horses, and probably those who had made the smoke a fiew days passed towards the S.W.

[Clark] *July 22, 1806*

I sent Sergt. Pryor and Shabono in serch of the horses with directions to proceed up the river as far as the 1st narrows and examine particularly for their tracks. They returned at 3 p.m. and informed me that they had proceeded up the distance I derected them to go and could see neither horses nor tracks. The plains imediately out from camp is so dry and hard that the track of a horse cannot be seen without close examination. I therefore derected Sergt. Pryor, Shannon, Shabono & Bratten to incircle the camp at some distance around and find the tracks of the horses and prosue them.

They serched for tracks all the evening without finding which course the horses had taken, the plains being so remarkably hard and dry as to render it impossible to see a track of a horse passing through the hard parts of them. I begin to suspect that they are taken by the Indians and taken over the hard plains to prevent our following them. My suspicions is grounded on the improbability of the horses leaveing the grass and rushes of the river bottoms of which they are very fond and taking imediately out into the open dry plains where the grass is but short and dry. If they had continued in the bottoms either up or down, their tracks could be followed very well. I directed Labeech who understands tracking very well to set out early in the morning and find what rout the horses had taken if possible.

[Clark] July 23, 1806

Last night the wolves or dogs came into our camp and eat the most of our dryed meat which was on a scaffold. Sgt. Pryor found an Indian mockerson and a small piece of a roab. The mockerson worn out on the bottom & yet wet, and have every appearance of haveing been worn but a fiew hours before. Those Indian signs is conclusive with me that they have taken the 24 horses which we lost on the night of the 20th instant, and that those who were about last night were in serch of the ballance of our horses which they could not find as they had fortunately got into a small prarie serounded with thick timber in the bottom. Labeech returned haveing taken a great circle and informed me that he saw the tracks of the horses makeing off into the open plains and were by the tracks going very fast.

[Clark] July 25, 1806

At 4 P.M. [I] arived at a remarkable rock situated in an extensive bottom. . . . This rock I ascended and from it's top had a most extensive view in every direction. This rock which I shall call Pompy's Tower is 200 feet high and 400 paces in secumpherance and only axcessable on one side which is from the N.E. the other parts of it being a perpendicular clift of lightish coloured gritty rock. On the top there is a tolerable soil of about 5 or 6 feet thick covered with short grass. The Indians have made 2 piles of stone on the top of this tower. The nativs have ingraved on the face of this rock the figures of animals &c. near which I marked my name and the day of the month & year.

[Clark] August 2, 1806

About 8 a.m. this morning a bear of the large vicious species being on a sand bar raised himself up on his hind feet and looked at us as we passed down near the middle of the river. He plunged into the water and swam towards us, either from a disposition to attack't or from the cent of the meat which was in the canoes. We shot him with three balls and he returned to shore badly wounded.

In the evening I saw a very large bear take the water above us. I ordered the boat to land on the opposit side with a view to attcack't him when he came within shot of the shore. . . . I shot it in the head. The men hauled her on shore and proved to be an old shee which was so old that her tuskes had worn smooth, and much the largest feemale bear I ever saw.

[Clark] August 4, 1806

Musquetors excessively troublesom so much so that the men complained that they could not work at their skins for those troublesom insects. And I find it entirely impossible to hunt in the bottoms, those insects being so noumerous and tormenting as to render it imposseable for a man to continue in the timbered lands and our best retreat from those insects is on the sand bars in the river and even those situations are only clear of them when the wind should happen to blow which it did to day for a fiew hours in the middle of the day. The evenings nights and mornings they are almost [un]indureable particularly by the party with me who have no bears [biers] to keep them off at night, and nothing to screen them but their blankets which are worn and have maney holes.

The torments of those missquetors and the want of a suffice[n]cy of buffalow meat to dry, those animals not to be found in this neighbourhood, induce me to deturmine to proceed on to a more eliagiable spot on the Missouri below at which place the musquetors will be less troublesom and buffalow more plenty. . . . Wrote a note to Capt. Lewis informing him of my intentions and tied it to a pole which I had stuck in the point. . . . Musquetors were so abundant that we were tormented much worst than at the point. The child of Shabono has been so much bitten by the musquetors that his face is much puffed up & swelled.

[Clark] August 5, 1806

The musquetors was so troublesom to the men last night that they slept but very little. Indeed they were excessive troublesom to me. My musquetor bear [bier] has a number of small holes worn through [which] they pass in. I set out at an early hour intending to proceed to some other situation. I had not proceded on far before I saw a ram of the big horn animal near the top of a larbd. bluff. I assended the hill with a view to kill the ram. The musquetors was so noumerous that I could not keep them off my gun long enough to take sight and by that means missed.

[Clark] August 6, 1806

This morning a very large bear of [the] white species discovered us floating in the water and takeing us, as I prosume to be buffalow imediately plunged into the river and prosued us. I directed the men to be still. This animal came within about 40 yards of us and tacked about. We all fired into him without killing him, and the wind so high that we could not pursue him, by which means he made his escape to the shore badly wounded.

[Clark] August 9, 1806

The squaw brought me a large and well flavoured goose berry of a rich crimsin colour, and [a] deep purple berry of the large cherry of the current species which is common on this river as low as the Mandans. The engagees call it the Indian current.

[Clark] August 12, 1806

At meridian Capt. Lewis hove in sight with the party which went by way of the Missouri as well as that which accompanied him from Travellers Rest on Clarks river. I was alarmed on the landing of the canoes to be informed that Capt. Lewis was wounded by an accident. I found him lying in the perogue. He informed me that his wound was slight and would be well in 20 or 30 days. This information relieved me very much. I examined the wound and found it a very bad flesh wound, the ball had passed through the fleshey part of his left thy below the hip bone and cut the cheek of the right buttock for 3 inches in length and the debtb of the ball. Capt. L. informed me the accident happened the day before by one of the men Peter Crusat misstaking him in the thick bushes to be an elk. . . . This Crusat is near sighted and has the use of but one eye. He is an attentive industrious man and one whome we both have placed the greatest confidence in dureing the whole rout.

Reunited, the captains floated downriver to the Mandan Villages, their former winter quarters, where they greeted friendly chiefs like Black Cat and Big White. But now the party that had held firm all the way to the Pacific was beginning to disperse.

[Clark] August 15, 1806

Colter, one of our men, expressed a desire to join some trappers who offered to become shearers with [him] and furnish traps &c. The offer [was] a very advantagious one to him. His services could be dispenced with from this down and as we were disposed to be of service to any one of our party who had performed their duty as well as Colter had done, we agreed to allow him the privilage provided no one of the party would ask or expect a similar permission to which they all agreeed that they wished Colter every suckcess. . . . [18]

[Clark] August 17, 1806

Settled with Touisant Chabono for his services as an enterpreter the price of a horse and lodge purchased of him for public service in all amounting to 500$ 33 1/3 cents. . . . At 2 oClock we left our encampment after takeing leave of Colter who also set out up the river in company with Messrs. Dickson & Handcock. We also took our leave of T. Chabono, his Snake Indian wife and their child who had accompanied us on our rout to the pacific ocean in the capacity of interpreter and interprete[s]s.

T. Chabono wished much to accompany us in the said capacity if we could have provailed [upon] the Menetarre chiefs to dcend the river with us to the U. States. But as none of those chiefs of whoes language he was conversent would accompany us, his services were no longer of use to the U. States and he was therefore discharged and paid up. We offered to convey him down to the Illinois if he chose to go. He declined proceeding on at present, observing that he had no acquaintance or prospects of making a living below and must continue to live in the way he had done. I offered to take his little son, a butifull promising child who is 19 months old, to which they both himself & wife wer willing provided the child had been weened. They observed that in one year the boy wold be sufficiently old to leave his mother & he would then take him to me if I would be so freindly as to raise the child for him in such a manner as I thought proper, to which I agreed &c. [19]

After leaving the Mandan Villages, the party proceeded rapidly down the Missouri through country rich in wild game . . . but also the home of the Teton Sioux, the tribe that had so vexed the explorers on the trip upriver.

[Clark] August 29, 1806

I assended to the high country and from an eminance, I had a view . . . of a greater number of buffalow than I had ever seen before at one time. I must have seen near 20,000 of those animals feeding on this plain. I have observed that in the country between the nations which are at war with each other the greatest numbers of wild animals are to be found.

[Clark] August 30, 1806

Capt. Lewis is mending slowly. . . . I saw several men on horseback which with the help of a spie glass I found to be Indians on the high hills to the N.E. We landing on the S.W. . . . Imedeatily after landing about 20 Indians was discovered on an eminance a little above us on the opposite side. One of those men I took to be a French man from his [having] a blanket capote & a handkerchief around his head. Imediately after 80 or 90 Indian men all armed with fusees & bows & arrows came out of a wood on the opposite bank about ¼ of a mile below us. They fired off their guns as a salute. We returned the salute with 2 rounds. We were at a loss to deturmin of what nation those Indians were. From their hostile appearance we were apprehenvise they were Tetons. . . .

I deturmined to find out who they were without running any risque of the party and Indians, and therefore took three French men who could speak the Mahar Pania and some Seeoux. . . . Imedeately after I set out 3 young men set out from the opposite side and swam next me on the sand bar. . . . I then derected the man who could speak a fiew words of Seioux to inquire what nation or tribe they belong to. They informed me that they were Tetons and their chief was *Tartack-kah-sab-bar* or the Black Buffalow.

This chief I knew very well to be the one we had seen with his band at Teton River which band had attempted to detain us in the fall of 1804 as we ascended this river and with whome we wer near

comeing to blows. I told those Indians that they had been deef to
our councils and ill treated us as we assended this river two years
past, they they had abused all the whites who had visited them
since. I believe them to be bad people & should now suffer them to
cross to the side on which the party lay, and directed them to
return with their band to their camp, that if any of them come near
our camp we should kill them certainly . . . and after they had
informed the chief &c. as I suppose what we had said to them, they
all set out on their return to their camps back of a high hill.

7 of them halted on the top of the hill and blackguarded us, told
us to come across and they will kill us all. . . . One man walked
down the hill to meet us and invited us to land to which invitation
I paid no kind of attention. This man I knew to be the one who
had in the fall 1804 accompanied us 2 days and is said to be the
friend to the white people. After we passd him he returned on the
top of the hill and gave 3 strokes with the gun (*on the earth—this is
swearing by the earth*) he had in his hand. This I am informed is a
great oath among the Indians.

[Clark] September 3, 1806

We spied two boats & several men. Our party pleyed their ores
and we soon landed on the side of the boats. The men of [these] boats
saluted us with their small arms. I landed & was met by a Mr. James
Airs from Mackanaw by way of Prarie Dechien and St. Louis. This
gentleman is of the house of Dickson & Co. of Prarie de Chian who
has a licence to trade for one year with the Sieoux. He has 2 batteaux
loaded with merchendize for that purpose. This gentleman receved
both Capt. Lewis and my self with every mark of friendship. He was
himself at the time with a chill of the agu on him which he has had
for several days. Our first enquirey was after the president of our
country and then our friends and the state of the politicks of our
country &c. and the state [of] Indian affairs to all of which enquireys

Mr. Aires gave us as satisfactory information as he had it in his power to have collected in the Illinois which was not a great deel.

This gentleman informed us of maney changes & misfortunes which had taken place in the Illinois amongst others the loss of Mr. Cady Choteaus house and furniture by fire. For this misfortune of our friend Choteaus I feel my self very much concern &c. He also informed us that Gen. Wilkinson was the governor of the Louisiana and at St. Louis 300 of the American troops had been cantuned on the Missouri a fiew miles above its mouth. Some disturbance with the Spaniards in the Nackatosh [Natchitoches] Country is the cause of their being called down to that country. The Spaniards had taken one of the U. States frigates in the Mediteranean. Two British ships of the line had fired on an American ship in the port of New York, and killed the Capt.'s brother. 2 Indians had been hung in St. Louis for murder and several others in jale. And that Mr. Burr & Gen. Hambleton fought a duel, the latter was killed &c. &c.

I am happy to find that my worthy friend Capt. L's is so well as to walk about with ease to himself &c.

[Clark] September 4, 1806

At meridian we came too at Floyds Bluff below the enterance of Floyds River and assended the hill, with Capt. Lewis and several men. Found the grave had been opened by the nativs and left half covered. We had this grave completely filled up, and returned to the canoes and proceeded on. . . .

[Clark] September 6, 1806

A little above the Petite River de Seeoux we met a tradeing boat of Mr. Og. Choteaux [Auguste Chouteau] bound to the River Jacque to trade with the Yanktons. This boat was in care of a Mr. Henry Delorn. . . . We purchased a gallon of whiskey of this man (*promised to pay Choteau who would not receive any pay*) and gave to each man of the party a dram which is the first spiritious licquor which had been tasted by any of them since the 4 of July 1805.

[Clark] September 9, 1806

My worthy friend Capt. Lewis has entirely recovered. His wounds are heeled up and he can walk and even run nearly as well as ever he could.

[Clark] September 14, 1806

We met three large boats bound to the Yankktons and Mahars . . . all from St. Louis. Those young men received us with great friendship and pressed on us some whisky for our men, bisquet, pork and onions. . . . Our party received a dram and sung songs until 11 oClock at night in the greatest harmoney.

[Clark] September 17, 1806

At 11 a.m. we met a Captain McClellin late a Capt. of Artily. of the U. States Army assending in a large boat. This gentleman an acquaintance of my friend Capt. Lewis was somewhat astonished to see us return and appeared rejoiced to meet us. . . . This gentleman informed us that we had been long since given out [up] by the people of the U.S. generaly and almost forgotton. The president of the U. States had yet hopes of us.

[Clark] September 20, 1806

We saw some cows on the bank which was a joyfull sight to the party and caused a shout to be raised for joy at [blank in manuscript] p.m. We came in sight of the little French village Charriton (*Charrette*). The men raised a shout and sprung upon their ores and we soon landed opposit to the village.

Our party requested to be permited to fire off their guns which was alowed & they discharged 3 rounds with a harty cheer, which was returned from five tradeing boats which lay opposit the village.... We purchased of a citizen two gallons of whiskey for our party for which we were obliged to give eight dollars in cash, an imposition on the part of the citizen. Every person, both French and Americans seem to express great pleasure at our return, and acknowledged themselves much astonished in seeing us return. They informed us that we were supposed to have been lost long since, and were entirely given out by every person &c.

[Clark] September 21, 1806

At 4 p.m. we arived in sight of S. Charles. The party rejoiced at the sight of this hospitable village, plyed thear ores with great dexterity, and we soon arived opposit the town. This day being Sunday we observed a number of gentlemen and ladies walking on the bank. We saluted the village by three rounds from our blunderbuts and the small arms of the party, and landed near the lower part of the town. We were met by great numbers of the inhabitants.

[Clark] September 23, 1806

Decended to the Mississippi and down that river to St. Louis at which place we arived about 12 oClock. We suffered the party to fire off their pieces as a salute to the town. We were met by all the village and received a harty welcom from its inhabitants &c. Here I found my old acquaintance Majr. W. Christy who had settled in this town in a public line as a tavern keeper. He furnished us with store rooms for our baggage and we accepted of the invitation of Mr. Peter Choteau and took a room in his house. We payed a friendly visit to Mr. August Chotau and some of our old friends this evening.

[Clark] September 24, 1806

I sleped but little last night. However we rose early and commenced weighting our letters. Capt. Lewis wrote one to the presidend and I wrote Govr. Harrison & my friends in Kentucky. . . . We dined with Mr. Chotoux today, and after dinner went to a store and purchased some clothes, which we gave to a tayler and derected to be made. Capt. Lewis in opening his trunk found all his papers wet, and some seeds spoiled.

[Clark] September 25, 1806

Had all of our skins &c. suned and stored away in a storeroom of Mr. Caddy Choteau. Payed some visits of form, to the gentlemen of St. Louis. In the evening a dinner & ball.

[Clark] September 26, 1806

A fine morning we commenced wrighting &c.[20]

---

1. The first reference to the fateful strategy of later splitting the party during the trip home. —LYJ
2. Moulton reports that this chief's name "referred to a red, or bleeding, grizzly bear," and that later whites called him the "Bloody Chief." As late as the 1840s he told whites of his meeting with Lewis and Clark. Moulton: "Nez Perce legend asserts that the sister of Red Grizzly Bear bore a son by William Clark. This man, who had light hair, was proud of his ancestry and would proclaim, 'Me Clark!' He was photographed at least once, in his old age, and was with the famous Nez Perce flight in 1877. Reportedly, a black child was also born after this expedition's passing but did not live to maturity." —LYJ
3. "Kooskooske" is usually the captains' name for present-day Clearwater; here the reference is to the Lochsa River in Idaho.
4. This area is now known as Lolo Hot Springs.
5. Moulton notes that "They were Piegans, members of one of the three main divisions of the Blackfeet confederation, the

other two being the Bloods and the Blackfeet proper." —LYJ

6. The place where Lewis encountered the Indians as on the south side of Two Medicine River, about four miles below the mouth of Badger Creek, on the eastern edge of the Blackfoot reservation. —Ed.

7. The name of the man killed was Side Hill Calf. The long-continued hostility of the Blackfeet to the whites has often been attributed to this incident. But Chittenden (*History of American Trade*) declares that Manuel Lisa found that the Indians of that tribe justified the action of Lewis, and were inclined to be friendly to whites. The real cause of the Blackfeet's enmity was the appearance of white trappers in the ranks of the enemies, the Crows, in a battle that occurred in 1807. It is noteworthy that Drouillard (Drewyer) finally lost his life in a contest with the Blackfeet. —Ed.

8. A short ax. —LYJ

9. Grog is a mixture of rum and water. —Moulton

10. These men, whom Clark met the previous day, were the first whites, outside their own party, whom the explorers had seen since the first winter at Fort Mandan. John Colter later persuaded the captains to let him join their trapping expedition to the Yellowstone River. —LYJ

11. This description of the pin cherry would be Lewis's last journal entry. —LYJ

12. The large creek from the right was the Pioneer, which heads up the east side of the same range of the Rockies as Fish Creek does on the west, and along whose course is now a pass called Big Hole. —Ed.

13. Near the encampment for this night was fought the Battle of Big Hole in the Nez Perce War, on August 9, 1877. The Indians under Chief Joseph escaped. —Ed.

14. Moulton identifies the plant as ternate, or nineleaf, lomatium. —LYJ

15. Opposite the site of the present town of Logan. —Ed.

16. Thwaites identifies the first pass noticed by Clark as the Bridger; Moulton says it was Flathead Pass in the Bridger Range. Sacagawea recommended the Bozeman Pass, the one later chosen for the Northern Pacific Railway and Interstate 90. —LYJ

17. The expedition reached the Yellowstone not far from the site of present-day Livingston, Montana. —Ed.

18. Colter was the one member of the voyage of discovery whose subsequent adventures were equally extraordinary. America's first mountain man, he discovered the marvels of the present-day Yellowstone National Park. After one spectacular escape from the Indians when, stripped naked, he successfully outran his pursuers, he returned to civilization in 1810 and died of jaundice in 1813. —Ed.

19. Clark repeated his offers to educate young "Pomp" and eventually, at the age of six, the boy moved into Clark's home in St. Louis. Jean-Baptiste later traveled to Europe with Prince Paul of Wurttemburg, then returned to the frontier as a mountain man and fur trader, serving as a guide for explorers and soldiers such as John C. Fremont. He died in Oregon in 1866. —Ed.

20. Lewis worked on a 3,200-word letter, eventually published in the newspapers, describing the journey. Clark may have been completing some entries in the journals. —LYJ

LETTER FROM
LEWIS TO JEFFERSON

Sir,

It is with pleasure that I anounce to you the safe arrival of myself and party at 12 OClk. today at this place with our papers and baggage. In obedience to your orders we have penitrated the continent of North America to the Pacific Ocean, and sufficiently explored the interior of the country to affirm with confidence that we have discovered the most practicable rout which dose exist across the continent by means of the navigable branches of the Missouri and Columbia rivers. Such is that by way of the Missouri to the foot of the rapids five miles below the great falls of that river a distance of 2575 miles, thence by land passing the Rocky Mountains to a navigable part of the Kooskooske[1] 340; with the Kooskooske 73 mls. a southeasterly branch[2] of the Columbia 154 miles and the latter river 413 mls. to the Pacific Ocean; making the total distance from the confluence of the Missouri and Mississippi to the discharge of the

198

Columbia into the Pacific Ocean 3555 miles. The navigation of the Missouri may be deemed safe and good; its difficulties arise from its falling banks, timber imbeded in the mud of it's channel, it's sand bars and steady rapidity of it's current, all which may be overcome with a great degree of certainty by taking the necessary precautions. The passage by land of 340 miles from the Missouri to the Kooskooske is the most formidable part of the tract proposed across the continent; of this distance 200 miles is along a good road, and 140 over tremendious mountains which for 60 mls. are covered with eternal snows; however a passage over these mountains is praticable from the latter part of June to the last part of September, and the cheep rate at which horses are to be obtained from the Indians of the Rocky Mountains and west of them, reduces the expences of transportation over this portage to a mere trifle. The navigation of the Kooskooske, the south east branch of the Columbia itself is safe and good from the 1ˢᵗ of April to the middle of August, by making three portages on the latter; the first of which in descending is that of 1200 paces at the great falls of the Columbia, 261 mls. from the ocean, the second of two miles at the long narrows six miles below the falls, and the 3ʳᵈ also of 2 miles at the great rapids 65 miles still lower down. The tides flow up the Columbia 183 miles, or within seven miles of the great rapids, thus far large sloops might ascend in safety, and vessels of 300 tons burthen could with equal safety reach the entrance of the river Multnomah,[3] a large southern branch of the Columbia, which taking it's rise on the confines of the Mexico with the Callardo and Apostles river, dischrages itself onto the Columbia 125 miles from it's mouth. From the head of the tide water to the foot of the long narrows the Columbia could be most advantageously navigated with large batteauxs, and from thence upwards by perogues. The Missouri possesses sufficient debth of water as far as is specifyed for boats of 15 tons burthen, but those of smaller capacity are to be prefered.

We view this passage across the continent as affording immence advantages to the fur trade, but fear that the advantages which it offers as a communication for the productions of the Eaest Indies to the United States and thence to Europe will never be found equal on an extensive scale to that by way of the Cape of Good Hope; still we believe that many articles not bulky brittle nor of a very perishable nature may be conveyed to the United States by this rout with more facility and at less expence than by that at present practiced.

The Missouri and all it's branches from the Cheyenne upwards abound more in beaver and common otter, than any other streams on earth, particularly the proportion of them lying within the Rocky Mountains. The furs of all this immence tract of country including such as may be collected on the upper portion of the river St. Peters, Red River and the Assinniboin with the immence country watered by the Columbia by the 1ˢᵗ of August in each year and from thence be shipped to, and arrive in Canton earlier than the furs at present shipped from Montreal annually arrive in London. . . .

Although the Columbia dose not as much as the Missouri abound in beaver and otter, yet it is by no means despicable in this rispect, and would furnish a valuable fur trade distinct from any other consideration in addition to the otter and beaver which it could furnish. There might be collected considerable quantities of the skins of three species of bear affording a great variety of colours and of superior delicacy, those also of the tyger cat, several species of fox, martin and several others of an inferior class of furs, besides the valuable sea otter of the coast.

If the government will only aid, even in a very limited manner, the enterprize of her citizens I am fully convinced that we shal shortly derive the benifits of a most lucrative trade from this source, and that in the course of ten or twelve years a tour across the continent by the rout mentioned will be undertaken by individuals with as little concern as a voyage across the Atlantic is at present. . . .

As a sketch of the most prominent features of our perigrination since we left the Mandans may not be uninteresting, I shall indeavour to give it to you by way of letter from this place, where I shall necessarily be detained several days in order to settle with and discharge the men who accompanyed me on the voyage as well as to prepare for my rout to the City of Washington.

We left Fort Clatsop where we wintered near the entrance of the Columbia on the 27th of March last, and arrived at the foot of the Rocky Mountains on the 10th of May where we were detained untill the 24th of June in consequence of the snow which rendered a passage over those mountains impracticable untill that moment; had it not been for this detention I should ere this have joined you at Montichello. In my last communication to you from the Mandans I mentioned my intention of sending back a canoe with a small party from the Rocky Mountains; but on our arrival at the great falls of the Missouri on the 14th of June 1805, in view of that formidable snowey barrier, the discourageing difficulties which we had to encounter in making a portage of eighteen miles of our canoes and baggage around those falls were such that my friend Capt. Clark and myself conceived it inexpedient to reduce the party, lest by doing so we should lessen the ardor of those who remained and thus hazard the fate of the expedition, and therefore declined that measure, thinking it better that the government as well as our friends should for a moment feel some anxiety for our fate than to wrisk so much; experience has since proved the justice of our dicision, for we have more than once owed our lives and the fate of the expedition to our number, which consisted of 31 men.

I have brought with me several skins of the sea otter, two skins of the native sheep of America, five skins and skelitons complete of the bighorn or mountain ram, and a skin of the mule deer beside the skins of several other quadrupeds and birds of natives of the countries through which we passed. I have also preserved a pretty extensive collection of plants, and collected nine other vocabularies.

I have prevailed on the great chief of the Mandan nation to accompany me to Washington;[4] he is now with my friend and colligue Capt. Clark at this place, in good health and sperits, and very anxious to proceede.

With rispect to the exertions and services rendered by that esteemable man Capt. William Clark in the course of late voyage I cannot say too much; if sir, any credit be due for the success of that arduous enterprize in which we have been mutually engaged, he is equally with myself entitled to your consideration and that of our common country.

The anxiety which I feel in returning once more to the bosom of my friends is a sufficient guarantee that no time will be unnecessarily expended in this quarter.

I have detained the post several hours for the purpose of making you this haisty communication. I hope that while I am pardoned for this detention of the mail, the situation in which I have been compelled to write will sufficiently apologize for having been this laconic. . . .

I am very anxious to learn the state of my friends in Albemarle particularly whether my mother is yet living. I am with every sentiment of esteem your obt. and very humble servant.

Meriwether Lewis
Capt. 1ˢᵗ U.S. Regt. Infty.

N.B. The whole of the party who accompanyed me from the Mandans have returned in good health, which is not, I assure you, to me one of the least pleasing considerations of the voyage.
M.L.

1. The Clearwater River —LYJ
2. The Snake River —LYJ
3. Today's Willamette River —LYJ
4. Lewis's party to Washington, D.C., from St. Louis included Clark, York, Ordway, Labiche, Pierre Choteau and a delegation of Osage chiefs, the Mandan chief Sheheke ("Big White") and his wife and son, and interpreter Rene Jusseaume and his wife and two children. As Donald Jackson reports in his *Letters of the Lewis & Clark Expedition* (University of Illinois, 1962), Jefferson welcomed Sheheke and the others in a speech dated December 30, 1806. After much difficulty, Sheheke was returned to his native village and died in 1832.